LAUGHING BLUES

The lost plays and other unproduced works

of

E. Alan Blackman

Norcor Enterprises
Chicago

ISBN 978-0-9622469-2-0

Printed in the United States of America

I laughed the day that I was born
and laughed again the day I died,
but the threescore years and ten between
left me most unsatisfied.

CONTENTS

Introduction

Everyone has their own notion of what constitutes humor which admittedly changes over time with cultural norms as well as levels of sophistication. Which begs the question: what is humor, and does it have a distinctive or universal trait, irrespective of time or place. Webster defines it as anything that appears ludicrous or appeals to the comic sense. But what appears ludicrous or appeals to the comic sense is as varied as its intended audience. At the very least it requires a shared experience, a pratfall or disconnect that the target audience can relate to. But most important, it must flatter by providing a sense of superiority, a mental perch as it were, to look down on the quandaries and miscues of its hapless victims.

Then there is time, said to be the arch enemy of all humor. What was funny on Tuesday may not be funny on Wednesday. Time brings new challenges and with them a whole new set of conundrums for the savvy humorist or jokesmith to toy with. Topical humor may be the bread and butter of standup comics but it is poison to the astute humorist who takes a more sweeping view of human foibles, be it a Mark Twain, Oscar Wilde, or even Mae West with her bawdy double-entendres. For them, what was true on Tuesday is still true on Wednesday. When Winston Churchill is accused of being drunk by an ugly lady parliamentarian, he retorts by saying that by morning he will be sober but she will still be ugly. The 'morning' could be any morning; it has no reference to anything but his sobriety and her ugliness. It is, in a word, timeless.

1

For the record, *Laughing Blues* makes no such claim. The title does, in fact, hint at self-parody, since much of the collection was indeed 'lost' or remains 'unproduced.' The material spans a good part of the 20th century with its branded turbulence and upheaval and which, for better or worse, provides the basis for much of the humor. But the patina of time is just as apt to render some of it anachronistic by today's standards. Accordingly, some of the included works require an awareness of a specific time and place to give it perspective. A case in point is *Invitation to a Russian Wake* which is a spoof on Russian communism written prior to its fall in 1991 and which assumes some familiarity with the period as well as with the bureaucratic mindset. Another example is *Our Declining Prestige* written at the height of the Vietnam War when "hate America" campaigns were de rigueur, especially in Europe. But it also helps to know that the now defunct "Saturday Evening Post" was very much alive, as was card-carrying prostitution in Paris. A third example is the performance piece *I thought I was in love with Nietzsche* which chronicles the morbidly precocious mutterings of one Pamela Crankshaft but which, for maximum effect, rests on having some exposure to a popular band leader of the day.

There is also the bugaboo of political correctness, especially as it applies to ethnic humor which, even in its most innocuous form, is now looked upon with disdain. What is lost in the process is the vitality and singularity of ethnics, leaving us with a dreary sameness that is not without its own hint of snobbery. *School for Sympathy*, a satire on our obsession with beauty, was written at a time when Yiddish humor was still an affordable option for comics. Like most Yiddish humor, *School for Sympathy* relies heavily on dialect, the lead character, convinced that beauty is a detriment to happiness, opts for ugliness, and does it with the fractured syntax and malapropisms of the set genre. No person or group is demeaned in the process. The dialect serves merely to embellish, further complicating a person's efforts to achieve success in a hopelessly misguided venture.

Along with changing attitudes and colloquialisms, time impacts humor in still other ways, not the least of which is changing monetary values. The purchasing power of a dime may seem far-fetched but it's diminution in value left *Poor Pigeon,* a sketch with Chaplinesque overtones, with nowhere to go since its effectiveness depended on the price of coffee being within reach of a panhandler's expectations, then nominally priced at ten cents a cup. The sheer ludicrousness of having a panhandler beg for a latte at $5 a cup may have its own humorous potential but the issues at stake in *Poor Pigeon* were the exaggerated importance attached to small sums, and the victim's misfortune of not having the right change. The problem was solved—hopefully—in a later rewrite by dispensing with actual denominations and substituting monetary equivalents instead, thereby restoring credibility to the panhandler's insistence on keeping the handout at the initial asking price.

Other included works seem less susceptible to the vagaries of time, though some readers may beg to differ. *Beyond the Gas* concerns an obsessive-compulsive couple with mutually conflicting needs that take them over the edge, all the while grappling intellectually with existential issues that are plainly out of their reach. *My, but wasn't that a Cold Summer!*, written in a similar vein, is about a problematic encounter of the third kind, a mother and daughter team, two loonies from the boonies pontificating on matters so out of their orbit they eventually go into one—at least metaphorically.

In a deliberate attempt to create a theatre piece devoid of plot, structure or conflict—in defiance of the so-called holy trinity of drama—I fashioned what is essentially an anti-play, a formless, plotless, semi-coherent piece entitled *Centrifuge,* relying on the ramblings of four disparate beings to carry the no-action plot forward. The sketch has never been performed or proffered for production (meaning, also, that it has never been rejected) so it is impossible to know if this act of dramatic defiance would work in a live setting.

In addition to *I thought I was in love with Nietzsche* I included two other performance pieces (they are too long to be classed as monologues). Both *Nibblets* and *The Meaning of Life* share a common trait. They are the perorations of seasoned rogues, one a gadfly poet, reflecting impishly on oddball characters he once knew, the other an aging pitchman peddling body parts at a Polygrip and Spare Body Parts convention. Both involve story-telling around a single theme and rely on situation humor, a more demanding art form as it calls for an attentiveness not required of other comedy formats.

In fairness to the reader, some of the selections *have* been produced or showcased in venues, both traditional and bizarre. *Orange Pekoe on the Rocks* was used as a lead-in to a musical revue that satirized the appearance of niceness as a cover for the dark underbelly of the human psyche. *You will tell Rodney*, cut from the same thematic cloth, was originally intended as a spoof on old-time soap operas but took an unexpected detour into dark humor, also masking the true nature of its main characters. *Poor Li'l Crocodile* is a story in itself, not only in the way it came about, but how it became a metaphor for the person who performed it.

It's the one work I drafted specifically on request, in this case a young actress who needed material for a local theatre fund-raiser. Being somewhat of a gadfly, she wanted something over-the-top, but funny, which morphed into a sleazy over-the-hill booze hound waxing philosophically—at times profanely—while fending off a bothersome fly which she dubs a crocodile and which, in the end, she slays with a fly swatter in much the same way her own life had been quashed by fate. The monologue, while implicitly poignant, was performed with such sluttish eloquence, it became an instant hit and a staple for the actress who performed it in a wide range of venues including, to my astonishment, a nunnery connected with Chicago's Holy Name Cathedral. But the story has a sad ending. The actress eventually left Chicago and returned to her home in Nebraska. Three years later I received news of her death from cancer at age 29. One can scoff at the irony but life does on occasion imitate art—sometimes with a vengeance.

I debated whether I should include *Street Unnamed* in this collection as it is neither comedic nor, in my judgment, good theatre. It is far too melodramatic and derivative of other works of its day and shows the strong influence of both Eugene O'Neill and Tennessee Williams. But it, too, has a somewhat storied beginning, being critiqued by the eminent New York drama critic and anthologist, John Gassner, whose class I attended but whose critique I was mercifully spared due to a funeral I attended the day of the reading. I had another play critiqued by Mr. Gassner a year later, only it wasn't my play he was critiquing. He kept referring to traces of Faulkner who I barely heard of at the time, much less read. When I suggested that he was possibly critiquing someone else's play, he did what for him must have been an agonizing recall (he was a play reader for the Theatre Guild and admitted to having read hundreds of plays in his day, most of them presumably as forgettable as mine). Years later I attended a lecture of his at the Goodman Theatre. On his leaving, I introduced myself as a former student only to be greeted with a blankness that was palpably numbing. His memory was no better then than it had been years earlier.

I list *Street Unnamed* (later changed to *Vista of Nameless Folk* to distinguish it from a movie released a year later entitled *The Street with no Name*) as a 'lost' play in the tradition of *Lost Plays of Eugene O'Neill*, not to put myself in his league—though his 'lost' plays exhibit some of the same flaws—but as a way of providing developmental insight into a dramatist's oeuvre. Coincidently, my first play (truly lost as I have no copy of it) was produced on the same bill as O'Neill's *Where the Cross is Made*, a dramatic pairing for which I was awarded $5 in war stamps! Also lost in the shuffle of time: two earlier titles (alas, non copyrightable), *So You Want to be President (1972)*, used as a title years later for a popular children's book, and another play (also lost) entitled *One Life to Live (1947)* which is now the title of a popular daytime soap. Need more be said about the plight of unsung authors?

But all this is prologue to what I hope will give pleasure to those who can laugh at the written word, while imagining how it might have sounded on some long-ago, forgotten stage. The material was deemed not good enough for the prescient arbiters of public taste but too good, in my unprescient opinion, to let die without a final viewing.

School for Sympathy

CHARACTERS

DR. HOPSNELL, *a renown quack & cosmetologist*

A FAT FAKE, *a glamorous wannabe*

OUR SADIE, *a Dracula wannabe*

THE SCENE: *The office of Dr. Hopsnell*

School for Sympathy

SCENE: *The office of DR. HOPSNELL, clearly identified by a large sign on the rear wall reading "Dr. Hopsnell's School of Beauty." Office furnishings include a desk and two chairs, one of them bearing an open portfolio. The desk is loaded with a mishmash of items used in the trade, including a jar of cold cream, a large vanity mirror, bottles of kelp and seaweed, an oversized plastic syringe, and, off to one side, a clipboard with several loose papers.*

The action begins with DR. HOPSNELL admonishing one of his more corpulent clients. She listens attentively, her mouth wide open, eagerly trying to comprehend.

HOPSNELL:
So in the summing up, there are several different kinds of proteins...

CLIENT [*foggishly*]:
Aaaah?

HOPSNELL:
And I don't want you to mix them.

CLIENT:
Aaaah?

HOPSNELL:
Whaddaya mean "Aaaah?" Don't say 'Aaaah.' You're overweight. We gotta get you down to two hundred—if you wanna be glamorous. You wanna be glamorous?

CLIENT [*nodding affirmatively*]:
Aaaah.

HOPSNELL:
Then shut up your mouth. You can't go around saying "Aaaah" all the time. People will think that you're stupid.

CLIENT:
Aaaah?

HOPSNELL [*grabbing a paper from the desk, demonstrating*]:
Now this is what you should eat on the list here—in red pencil. And this is what I am against because why—why am I against this list?

CLIENT:
Aaaah?

HOPSNELL [*as if to a child*]:
Because it ain't protein!

CLIENT [*brightening*].
Aaaah!

HOPSNELL:
Now you go home and you work some on the dumbbells.

CLIENT:
Ah-hah.

HOPSNELL:
And the exercycle.

CLIENT:
Ah-hah.

HOPSNELL:
And on Tuesday, I'll see you on Tuesday—if you can make it. Can you make it?

CLIENT [*assuringly*]:
Aaaah.

HOPSNELL:
Through the door, I mean?

CLIENT [*not so assuringly*]:
Aaaah.

HOPSNELL:
We'll make you out like Sophie Loren—in six months—with cellulose.

CLIENT [*departing*]:
Aaaah.

HOPSNELL [*following her to the door, shouting*]:
The miracle drug of science!

CLIENT [*off*]:
Aaaah.

HOPSNELL [*aside*]:
With you it can't be anything else—*but* a miracle! [*Turning back, wiping his brow.*] Oy, what a discussion! Six appointments and not one word but 'Aaaah' in eighty-nine different ways. [*Gathering up some papers from the desk and stuffing them into the portfolio.*] I'm giving up, and that's no fiction. In one sitting I should make a punchbowl into a cocktail glass. Not a simple chintzy piece of glass with a stem but a Speisman Engel with a svelte pinge. What I would give for a creature, for one single creature who don't wanna be a clown in the circus with

10

Turkish cigarettes and a mantilla, who could walk in and say "Dr. Hopsnell, I don't wanna be a schnootzie tootsie. Just make me out like I am, with my natural radiance. Bring it out, what's inside. Don't make me like something I'm not."

[*SADIE enters with a flourish. She is a guileless creature, middle-aged, but with the exuberance of a child, sweetly attractive and stunningly dressed. She deposits an oversized bundle on the empty chair, along with her purse, then removes her gloves.*]

SADIE [*while entering; as if on cue*]:
I don't wanna be a schnootzie tootsie. Just make me out like I am, with my natural radiance—

HOPSNELL [*barely looking up; stuffing more papers in the port.*]:
It's no use. I'm closing the gate.

SADIE [*extending her hand, expecting it to be kissed*]:
Dr. Hopsnell, a pleasure. An absolute pleasure!

HOPSNELL [*ignoring the gesture, but pausing to look at her hand*]:
What is it? You got a kink or something? It looks mangled

SADIE:
What is a kink?

HOPSNELL [*back to the port., more stuffing*]:
It is in you a pleasure but in me it's a pain. What is the problem?

SADIE [*taken aback*]:
Hah?

HOPSNELL:
You got a problem. What is it?

11

SADIE [*stammering*]:
I-I-I'm looking—

HOPSNELL:
You're looking?

SADIE:
For-for-for something like a school, approximately—

HOPSNELL [*without bothering to look up*]:
That's precisely what we are—approximately a school.

SADIE:
With a new kind of specialty for inside-out finishing.

HOPSNELL:
What you mean is a finishing school.

SADIE [*removing the bundle and purse from the chair; sits*]:
Not a finishing school. What I'm looking for like is a scraping-off
school—to bring out what is in me dying.

HOPSNELL:
You want out what is dying? I'm not a medical doctor.

SADIE:
You don't get me.

HOPSNELL:
I don't want you.

SADIE:
'Dying' is a figure of speech.

HOPSNELL:
I can see why it's dying.

SADIE:
It's not a physical dying. It's that something inside what is you—that schmeen of a peeschmod—

HOPSNELL:
Eh, what I would give for a peeschmod!

SADIE:
It don't sing in you. It don't cry in you. It don't rumble inside like it used to, so it must be dying.

HOPSNELL:
But it still rumbles a little?

SADIE [*with a trace of poignancy*]:
Like a voice, I can hear it. It calls to me, "Sadie, I'm here. Here I am, Sadie. Let me out."

HOPSNELL:
You're sure you don't want a medical doctor?

SADIE:
But I don't listen, see.

HOPSNELL:
You don't listen.

SADIE:
Because I don't have time for voices. I'm too involved in the world, vying for this and vying for that, living the part of a vivacious woman. Cocktail parties, book reviews, garden teas I'm giving four times a

week and fund raising for this and Travelers Aid on Saturday, running away from these voices what I'm doing—becoming a hard and callous woman—like a shell from Harper's Bazaar. The real me, I keep looking. Where is it? Gone. Swept up in the whirlwind of life. I look at myself in the mirror. What I see is not Sadie but a shell of a woman—still beautiful, yes, on the outside, but a shell. [*With growing poignancy.*] And who really cares? That's what I'm saying—to myself I'm saying that. Who can sympathize with a miserable shell?

HOPSNELL:
You're not getting sympathy?

SADIE:
Oy, what I'm getting.

HOPSNELL:
It's painful?

SADIE:
It's killing.

HOPSNELL:
People don't like you?

SADIE:
You don't have to believe it. I'm not asking you to believe it.

HOPSNELL:
It happened. A tragedy or something.

SADIE:
I'm not a sensitive woman. The slings and arrows I can handle with a shrug of a shoulder. The insolence of office I can chalk up to a vicissitude.

HOPSNELL:
What is the point you are making?

SADIE:
But it happened. Forty-five years in a parachute factory.

HOPSNELL:
You work in a parachute factory?

SADIE:
Forty-five years—on ripcords. But I'm happy, see, because today is for me a milestone. I am looking ahead for a big luncheon—maybe a speech what is a thank you kindly for lasting so long—if I'm lucky, a pension—or what is the least, a Lady Hamilton with 'Sadie' engraved.

HOPSNELL:
What did you get?

SADIE [*displaying the bundle on her lap*]:
A parachute. They told me to jump.

HOPSNELL:
That's not getting sympathy.

SADIE [*almost tearfully*]:
That's what I'm saying.

HOPSNELL:
Because you know why? You're not a real person, frankly.

SADIE:
You don't think so?

HOPSNELL:
Look at you. You're like a ten dollar floor wax. You got a high gloss but no grip. That's why you're losing out, because you don't have a grip.

SADIE:
That's what it is. I'm losing my grip.

HOPSNELL:
You take a ravishing woman. She can be sincere like an ox, but it don't show. Stand her along side of a Dracula and she don't have a chance.

SADIE:
Is that for a fact?

HOPSNELL:
It's a known impedium.

SADIE:
I had a sneaking suspicion.

HOPSNELL:
What you need is some texture, a little schklup, so people will look at you and say, "Oy, what a rough natural texture."

SADIE [*repeating with glee*]:
Oy, what a rough natural texture.

HOPSNELL:
So raw and simple, like a piece of nature.

SADIE:
What I would give for a piece of nature!

HOPSNELL:
To bring out the peeschmod in you so it will sing and cry and make a big rumble. [*Grabbing the clipboard, he sits opposite SADIE.*] What is the name?

SADIE [*stammering*]:
Sa-Sa-Sadie. Sadie Schmulkmeyer.

HOPSNELL [*setting the clipboard on his lap*]:
Schmulkmeyer I like, but not Sadie.

SADIE:
What's wrong with Sadie?

HOPSNELL:
It ain't got a lilt.

SADIE:
With Schmulkmeyer you want a lilt?

HOPSNELL:
From now on you're a Sybil.

SADIE:
Sybil Schmulkmeyer. Oy, what a name!

HOPSNELL;
You like it?

SADIE:
So authentic. It goes to the core.

HOPSNELL [*putting the clipboard aside, grabbing a fistful of hair*]:
We start with the hair, what is on you the coiffure. It's a misconception completely.

SADIE:
You think so?

HOPSNELL [*handing her the jar of cold cream*]:
Look at it. It's soft and silky. It's not for a Sybil. And take off the face.

SADIE;
I should take off the face?

And don't wash it for six months. And don't cut your fingernails. You're cutting your nails. I can't make you a Dracula if you cut your nails.

SADIE [*applying the cold cream to her face*]:
For six years I won't cut a finger.

HOPSNELL:
Pull off the dress. It's not you.

SADIE:
I'm slapping my face.

HOPSNELL [*grabbing the cold cream jar*]:
You call that a slap. Give me the cream.

SADIE [*starting to remove the dress*]:
What's wrong with the dress?

HOPSNELL [*slapping on the cream*]:
Shut up the mouth. I'm losing the cream.

SADIE:
Forty-five dollars at Kline's.

HOPSNELL:
Forget about Kline's. [*Singing.*] "I'm sailing along on Moonlight Bay. Oh, I'm sailing along on Moonlight Bay…!

[*HOPSNELL continues slapping to the beat of the lyrics, applying the cream to the dress as it is pulled over SADIE'S head. There is a quick fade out, denoting a passage of time. When the light returns SADIE is transformed into a grotesquery, her face and hair mangled beyond recognition, her undergarments a hanging garden of rips and tears.*

She assumes a crouched position while pondering her makeover in the vanity mirror.]

HOPSNELL [*gleefully*]:
What a mess! What a wonderful mess!

SADIE:
I'm pitiful?

HOPSNELL:
You're disgusting.

[*The fat CLIENT reappears at the door.*]

CLIENT [*pointing at the desk*]:
Aaaah.

HOPSNELL [*directed at the CLIENT*]:
For you there ain't even a synonym! What is it? You forgot your cellulose?

19

CLIENT (*continues pointing, but in a different direction*]:
Aaaah.

HOPSNELL:
You *didn't* forget your cellulose?

CLIENT [*now pointing to the bundle on the vacated chair*]:
Aaaah. Aaaah

HOPSNELL [*referring to the bundle*]:
Is this what you're after?

CLIENT [*nodding "yes"*]:
Aaaah-ha-ha-ah-ah-ah-ah-ah.

HOPSNELL [*offering her the bundle*]:
You can say that again!

[*She leaves with the bundle. HOPSNELL follows her to the door, picking up the giant syringe on the way and vigorously adjusting the plunger.*]

SADIE [*a bit apprehensive*]:
Dr. Hopsnell—

HOPSNELL [*at the door; turning briefly to SADIE*]:
Could you hold it a second.

SADIE [*putting the mirror down*]:
Frankly, I'm satisfied.

HOPSNELL [*calling out to the CLIENT*]:
The ripcord, sweetheart! It's sixty floors to the subway!

20

_____

[*A loud crash, off.*]

What a schlemiel!

SADIE:
She didn't make it?

HOPSNELL [*pitching the syringe*]:
Lucky she had a parachute.

SADIE [*into her purse*]:
So what do I owe you.

HOPSNELL [*with the wave of a hand*]:
Forget it. It was a pleasure.

SADIE:
You can't do it for pleasure.

HOPSNELL:
Then I'll do it for pain. As a matter of fact I can't stand even to look at you. It's so sad.

SADIE:
Then it's working?

HOPSNELL [*gripping his chest*]:
Like a chain saw. It's cutting me to pieces.

SADIE:
It's maybe what you call a sympathy pain?

HOPSNELL:
Offhand, I'd say it was closer to grief.

21

SADIE:
It takes from you your happiness?

HOPSNELL:
Who said I was happy. I'm a miserable creature.

SADIE:
The peeschmod, it don't sing in you?

HOPSNELL:
Not a sound on the pavement. Not even a rumble.

SADIE:
What a pity.

HOPSNELL:
Maybe it rumbles a little, but I don't listen.

SADIE:
You're too involved in the world.

HOPSNELL:
Precisely.

SADIE:
And who really cares.

HOPSNELL:
That's what I'm saying. To myself I'm saying that.

SADIE:
You're not getting sympathy.

HOPSNELL:
Oy, what I'm getting.

SADIE:
People don't like you.

HOPSNELL:
You don't have to believe it. I'm not asking you to believe it.

SADIE [*grabbing the jar of cold cream*]:
What is the name?

HOPSNELL [*pulling up a chair, sitting; almost tearfully*]:
Ziggy. Ziggy Hopsnell. Doctor of Culture.

[*SADIE dips her hand in the cold cream jar and starts slapping it on HOPSNELL'S face.*]

SADIE [*singing, while slapping with a frenzy*]:
"I'm sailing along on Moonlight Bay!…Oh, I'm sailing along on Moonlight Bay…!"

[*The scene dims to the 'splotching' sounds of cold cream and the lyrical abandon of OUR SADIE.*]

Our Declining Prestige

CHARACTERS

TWIPSEED

WAITER

A LADY CUSTOMER

MRS. TWIPSEED

THE SCENE: *A sidewalk café in Paris*

Our Declining Prestige

SCENE: *A sidewalk café in Paris consisting of two or three tables with chairs and an overhead sign reading "Café de Pigalle." A LADY CUSTOMER in tight-fitting shorts and high leather boots is sipping coffee at one of the tables.*

The action begins with the appearance of TWIPSEED, a dapper American male, about forty, who is greeted by a WAITER who approaches from the opposition direction. TWIPSEED is carrying a bulging briefcase.

WAITER:
Bon jour, Monsieur Twipseed.

TWIPSEED [*extending his hand*]:
Bon jourey to you, you old rascal. How are ya?

WAITER [*wringing his hand after a forceful shake*]:
Madam Twipseed is not with you today?

TWIPSEED:
Oh, she'll be along. Has her little project, you know. Lots of Parisians still floating around, have to be interrogated.

WAITER:
She is still on ze project?

TWIPSEED [*crossing to a table next to the LADY CUSTOMER*]:
You know Mrs. Twipseed. She doesn't stop with the facts. I mean she's really going into this thing in a deep way.

OUR DECLINING PRESTIGE

WAITER [*offering a menu to TWIPSEED who is now seated*]:
She is strong on ze psychology, eh?

TWIPSEED:
Oh, god, yes. Motivation is everything. Without motivation—well, forget it because it won't sell. [*Catching the eye of the LADY CUSTOMER; smiling back toothily.*] Hi!

WAITER:
You are having ze usual, Monsieur?

TWIPSEED [*with eyes still fixed on the LADY CUSTOMER*]:
What? Oh, you mean the usual. Ha-ha! [*Back to the menu.*] I-don't-know-if-I-should. I mean these exotic blends—I suppose they're alright for tourists but then, golly gee whiz, I've been here long enough to have American coffee.

WAITER [*taking the menu; a slight bow*]:
Oui, Monsieur.

TWIPSEED [*to the WAITER who has started off*].
And, garkahn…make that with sugar, will you please.

[*Another slight bow and the WAITER leaves. TWIPSEED places his briefcase on the table and removes some papers.*]

[*To the LADY CUSTOMER.*] Frankly, I get so furious with Americans. I mean they leave the country and they're just deathly afraid of looking like tourists—and, god knows, you can tell. [*She smiles.*] I don't know why Americans should be ashamed of—well, to put it bluntly—*being* Americans. I'm not saying we're perfect, but then, heaven knows, who is. We've been leaning over backwards trying to be the good neighbor and everybody hates us. I know because my wife is taking a survey and it's shocking. I mean our prestige has never been lower.

27

LADY CUSTOMER:
Presteezhe?

TWIPSEED:
It is amazing. I mean I've got all the evidence right here. Papers and papers of documented, honest-to-goodness statements from the lips of foreigners—about our prestige. Why wife has spent six months *walking* the streets of Paris.

LADY CUSTOMER:
Ah! She is walking?

TWIPSEED:
Night and day.

LADY CUSTOMER [*with heightened interest*]:
Oh. She has a card?

TWIPSEED:
Oh, god, she's got a million of them. She's with the Associated Press for one thing— [*The WAITER returns with coffee.*] Thanks a lot. But this thing that she's doing, it's being done by the Post—Saturday Evening, that is.

[*The WAITER exits.*]

LADY CUSTOMER:
Monsieur, you are teasing.

TWIPSEED:
No, really, it's a fact.

LADY CUSTOMER:
She is doing it by the post on Saturday?

TWIPSEED:
She's completely laid out. It's simply a question of how much they can take. I don't have to tell you it's going to be shocking.

LADY CUSTOMER:
The poleece, they are not stopping her?

TWIPSEED:
Actually, she's had a greater response from them as a group—

LADY CUSTOMER:
No, Monsieur, I can't believe that.

TWIPSEED:
No, really. There wasn't a sour apple in the bunch.

LADY CUSTOMER:
My god, we would be shot for doing what she is doing.

TWIPSEED:
Actually, she's doing a lot more than she has to. There's three million people in Paris and I think she's sampled at least twenty percent.

LADY CUSTOMER:
No! That is impossible.

TWIPSEED:
Let's face it. She has an enormous capacity for work.

LADY CUSTOMER [*clasping her hands in glee*]:
I lohve that! So blasé, you Americans. You do always the extraordinary and you theenk nothing of it.

TWIPSEED:
I don't know that it's so extraordinary. It has been done before.

LADY CUSTOMER:
But on such a grand scale! I don't know how she can do it.

TWIPSEED:
You don't know my wife. She never lets up, even for a sweet roll.

LADY CUSTOMER:
I can't believe that. She has to have a pause now and then.

TWIPSEED:
She will have an occasional cigarette.

LADY CUSTOMER [*slapping her chest in feigned relief*]:
Oh, thank god!

TWIPSEED:
Mind you, it's not habitual or anything.

LADY CUSTOMER:
I lohve it when you are like that. You Americans, you are all so broadminded. You can do anything and nobody cares.

TWIPSEED:
Well, it is a democracy.

LADY CUSTOMER:
She can be walking the streets and you don't mind.

TWIPSEED [*a pause marking a belated epiphany*]:
Now, wait a minute. I mean—just a minute here.

30

LADY CUSTOMER [*more clasping of hands*]:
I lohve that! I lohve you when you are like that.

TWIPSEED [*indignantly*]:
My wife is with The Saturday Evening Post.

LADY CUSTOMER:
That's why I mean. She can do anything.

TWIPSEED:
Oh, I mean, really. This is embarrassing. There's been a dreadful mistake here, actually, and I don't know how to say it. It's apparent there's been a breakdown in communications here someplace because—well—let's face it: My wife is not a streetwalker.

LADY CUSTOMER:
She is not a streetwalker?

TWIPSEED:
I mean she does walk the streets, yes, but not in that sense. At least I hope not. God forbid, our prestige is bad enough as it is.

LADY CUSTOMER:
You don't approve of walking the streets?

TWIPSEED:
Well, I mean, after all—

LADY CUSTOMER [*overlapping*]:
It has no presteezhe, is that what you are saying? They are not high enough on the scale for you?

TWIPSEED:
Well, look at them. They're—they're pigs, most of them.

31

LADY CUSTOMER:
PEEGS?!

TWIPSEED:
Well, I, don't say all of them are.

LADY CUSTOMER:
I am a streetwalker, did you know that?

TWIPSEED [*smitten*]:
No kidding? Ha-ha! You're joking.

Hereinafter the STREETWALKER:
Now, what do you theenk? Do I look like a peeg?

TWIPSEED:
Well, for cryin' out loud, why didn't you say so. Ha-ha!

STREETWALKER:
You theenk I am low and common?

TWIPSEED:
I didn't say that.

STREETWALKER:
I don't have presteezhe?

TWIPSEED:
Now, hold it a second—

STREETWALKER:
What do you know about presteezhe?!

TWIPSEED:
You don't have to get so traumatic about it.

STREETWALKER [*rising*]:
I am a womaan! I am a harlot on the street! I am as old as Jezebel!

TWIPSEED:
I'm not disputing that at all.

STREETWALKER [*starting to circle TWIPSEED'S table; with flam-buoyant gestures*]:
I am like perfume in the naaght! I give lohve—and hope—and comfort. If a man is poor, I make him rich. If he is old, I make him young. If he is sad, I make him lighthearteed!

TWIPSEED:
I'll go along with that. I mean it's really great what you're doing.

STREETWALKER:
In the naaght you can see them steal from their apartmince to where the lahts are dim. It is lohve they seek. And who givos them lohve? When they are alone and there ees no one who cares? [*Thumping her chest.*] The streetwalker, she geeves them lohve! And you say she has no presteezhe! She who has outlasted all the professions does not have presteezhe! You must be out of your mind with madness! [*Swinging her arm across the table, she sweeps several papers to the floor.*]

TWIPSEED [*starting for the papers*]:
Just a minute here now—you're spilling my papers.

STREETWALKER:
I know you. You live in a cuckoo house. You come from Schenectacudy or someplace.

TWIPSEED [*on his knees, gathering up the papers*]:
Now, really, that's going a bit too far.

STREETWALKER:
You are a slave of convention. You have a wife and six keeds and you are faithful.

TWIPSEED:
I'm glad you brought that up—

STREETWALKER:
You know nothing of life except what goes on in Schenectacudy.

TWIPSEED [*back on his feet*]:
First of all, I'm not from Schenectacud-sk-sk-Schenectady. I'm from Rutherford, New Jersey where there's just as much debauchery as there is here—frankly.

STREETWALKER:
Deebotcheree?

TWIPSEED:
Secondly, I have been around. [*Sitting.*] You talk about life and all that like I was a grade-A moron or something. I mean—like—well, take yourself for instance. I don't care what you are. If you want to walk the streets, far be it from me to impose my will on a fellow human being.

STREETWALKER [*returning to her table, sitting*]:
It's not your will. It's your attitude I don't lahk.

TWIPSEED [*moving his chair closer to hers*]:
Now wait a minute. I'm coming to that. You think because I'm from the U.S. of A. that I'm square like everybody else. Well, I got a surprise for you.

34

[*A woman wearing horn-rimmed glasses enters, unnoticed. She is recording something in a journal as TWIPSEED edges closer to the STREETWALKER.*]

I lived in a rooming house once that had twenty-nine bonafide streetwalkers—including the landlady—and if that isn't a prep school for life, I don't know what is. Whenever I go back I always stop for an evening, even if I have to leave my wife at a hotel—but it's worth it because they're really swell people. I mean, they're actually quite human which is more than I can say for my wife who I'll be very frank to admit is not my idea of a woman. She's got all the machinery and everything but the gears don't seem to mesh for some reason or other....I'll be very frank. There's nothing between us. I mean marriage is alright if there's something there, you know—after all, what *is* marriage but friendship sanctioned by the police—ha-ha!—but when it's completely defunct like ours obviously is, your absolutely right about your philosophy and everything; and I've been thinking very seriously about getting a divorce except that she's—well—supporting me. I mean I'm not a fool. I— [*TWIPSEED'S eyes catch the woman hovering near the table.*]

STREETWALKER:
What is wrong, Monsieur?

TWIPSEED [*stricken*]:
I—think—I'm—going—to—faint.

MRS. TWIPSEED [*crossing to position facing TWIPSEED*]:
Fainting is too good for you, you-you-you FUNGUS! The idea, my gears not meshing! What do you know about gears? You don't even know how to pick your own teeth, you swivel-minded parasite!

TWIPSEED:
Well, now really—

MRS. TWIPSEED:
"Marriage…friendship sanctioned by the police"—I like that! You should have your mouth washed—corrupting the mind of this poor innocent girl.

TWIPSEED:
Now, Hazel, if you'll just listen—

MRS. TWIPSEED:
I've played the fool long enough. You can go back to your twenty-nine streetwalkers—including the landlady—and rot as far as I'm concerned!

TWIPSEED:
It's absolutely, categorically untrue—what you're thinking.

MRS. TWIPSEED:
You can tell that to the judge.

TWIPSEED:
I mean if you think I carried on with some common, ordinary streetwalker—

STREETWALKER:
What do you mean, 'common'?

TWIPSEED:
I don't mean common exactly—

MRS. TWIPSEED:
But you did carry on. I heard you distinctly.

36

TWIPSEED:
Well, if I did, I didn't carry on in that sense. I mean I didn't actually touch them or anything.

STREETWALKER:
You don't touch them? What is this nonsense?

TWIPSEED:
Well, I *touched* them. I mean *maybe* I touched them. But I didn't actually play around.

MRS. TWIPSEED:
You touched a streetwalker?

TWIPSEED:
Well, maybe I did.

STREETWALKER:
Now eet's maybe.

MRS. TWIPSEED [*grabbing the briefcase*].
I've heard enough. Give me my briefcase, Henry.

TWIPSEED [*hanging on to the briefcase*]:
I mean the truth, if you want to know—

STREETWALKER:
It was a rooming house, I remember that.

TWIPSEED:
I don't even think there *was* a streetwalker.

STREETWALKER [*rising*]:
So!

37

TWIPSEED:
I mean I don't even think I know what I'm talking about. You got me so gosh-darned confused with my nervous headaches and everything.

STREETWALKER:
You Americans, you lie! All the time you are lying, I hate you. I hate Americans. They are lowdown on the scale and I hate them. [*She starts to leave.*]

MRS. TWIPSEED [*lights up*]:
You *hate* Americans?

STREETWALKER [*mockingly, in the manner of TWIPSEED*]:
I think they are peegs, actually.

MRS. TWIPSEED [*crossing to the STREETWALKER*]:
That's very interesting because I'm taking a survey on that very thing. I mean I've been walking the streets for the past six months trying to ascertain the extent of our prestige.

STREETWALKER [*wide-eyed*]:
You are walking?

MRS. TWIPSEED:
It's the only way to do it, actually. Let's face it, if you're going to meet the man on the street—

STREETWALKER [*grabbing her by the arm*]:
You've got to go to the street, I know. Come along.

[*They exit arm-in-arm.*]

TWIPSEED [*calling out*]:
Hazel, for god's sake! You'll do the same damn thing that I did. [*He*

takes a sip of his coffee, then sets the cup down; with a bitter expression.] Damn this American coffee!

[*The scene dims to black.*]

MY, BUT WASN'T THAT A

COLD SUMMER!

THE CHARACTERS

MAMA

LOLA, *her daughter*

THE SCENE: *A cold summer on the dotty edge*

My, But Wasn't That A Cold Summer!

SCENE: *Twilight. An aging mother and her bespectacled daughter are seated side-by-side on a white frame porch, facing downstage. MAMA is firmly wedded to a rocker, a fly swatter on her lap. LOLA, in hair curlers and lounging robe, poses vacantly into space, gripping a rolled-up magazine.*

The beginning is marked by a prolonged silence, punctuated only by the rhythmic motion of the rocker.

LOLA [*breaking the spell; with endearing solicitousness*]:
Are you cold, mama?

MAMA:
No.

LOLA:
You can have a shawl if you're cold.

[*MAMA'S only response is to hit the porch railing with the swatter.*]

What did you do that for, mama?

MAMA [*numbly*]:
There was a fly on the railing.

LOLA:
There was?

42

MY, BUT WASN'T THAT A COLD SUMMER!

[*MAMA resumes her rocking. Another period of silence.*]

MAMA:
Why is it so dark, Lola?

LOLA:
Because it's night, mama. It's getting nighttime.

MAMA:
The sun doesn't seem to wanna go down.

LOLA:
That ain't the sun, mama. That's the moon.

[*More rocking. LOLA fidgets with the magazine, rolling it tighter.*]

MAMA:
My tooth hurts.

LOLA:
Oh, shush on your old tooth. It doesn't hurt.

MAMA [*following a reflective pause*]:
Why doesn't my tooth hurt, Lola?

LOLA:
Because you don't have any teeth, that's why. You haven't had any teeth since before you were sixty. Dr. Hoskins pulled 'em out when you were in Davidson, remember—when we took you to Davidson to have your teeth out?

[*MAMA half-nods an acknowledgment. Looking away, LOLA resumes her oration as if to some third party in space.*]

LOLA:
You should remember that, mama. That was the year when we had such a late summer and it was cold like this one. It was a cold, late summer when we went to Davidson—that year that you had your teeth out. I thought it would never come, with the temperature down in the 40's, all summer long it was cold except for that spell in August when it came finally, the summer, after being so cold.

MAMA:
Wasn't that a cold summer, though.

LOLA:
That's what I said, mama. It was cold.

MAMA:
And so late.

LOLA [*peering outward from above her glasses*]:
Mr. Peabody is home early from the grange. There was nobody there, I bet.

[*MAMA swats the railing a second time.*]

You killed that fly once, mama.

MAMA:
I did?

LOLA:
Yes, you did. [*Relieving MAMA of the swatter.*] They have all that planting to do yet in the fields.

MAMA:
Huh?

44

LOLA:
That's why there was nobody at the grange, because they have all that planting to do yet. The frost was so late getting out of the ground…I say, the frost was late getting out of the ground.

[*She elicits a perfunctory nod from MAMA who appears more focused on a problem she is having with the rocker.*]

What *are* you doin', mama?

MAMA:
It's stuck here, or somthin'.

LOLA:
No, it ain't stuck. It's your imagination. You're sure you don't want a shawl?

MAMA:
No.

LOLA:
You can have one if you want.

MAMA [*with a trace of irritation*]:
I said 'no.'

LOLA:
The wind is from the northeast. That's why you're having such a time with your rocker. Because you're rockin' against the wind.

MAMA:
I don't feel any wind.

LOLA:
I don't suppose you would with your numbness which I dare say has gotten worse ever since your bout with the chilblains.

MAMA:
I had the chilblains?

LOLA:
My lord, I hope to tell you, you had the chilblains.

MAMA:
Was that the time we went to Davidson?

LOLA:
No, that was another summer.

MAMA:
Was that as cold—?

LOLA:
No, mama. It was not as cold as that summer we went to Davidson. There was no summer that was that cold...Almost as cold, but not that cold.

MAMA:
Then why did I get the chilblains?

LOLA [*sharply*]:
How do I know why you got the chilblains. I presume it's because you didn't have the resistance. The Lord didn't make us to last forever. [*Refolding her robe at the knees.*] It's amazing we lasted this long, considering...Mama, what *are* you doin', doin', doin'?

46

MAMA [*picking up an object from the floor*]:
I thought so. It was a piece of glass from the time we had the lemonade.

LOLA:
You mean the glass that you broke—that you dropped on your foot with the missing toe. That was two summers ago. That can't be the same glass.

MAMA:
It looks like the same glass.

LOLA [*taking the object from MAMA*]:
Let's see. No, that's not the same glass. That had a blue tint to it. This is more yellow.

MAMA:
I didn't know I had a toe missing.

LOLA:
That's because you don't look at your toes anymore. I do all the trimmin'. No, it was a blue one that you broke.

MAMA:
A blue one? I had a blue toe?

LOLA:
No, mama. The glass. You never had a toe. That toes was missing from when you were born. It was like a mutation, when people are born without all the pieces.

MAMA:
I wonder why that is?

LOLA:
I guess it's because the Lord has to make so many people He doesn't have time to finish the job. [*Perusing the glass object.*] I'd sure like to know where this is from, though. You didn't break another glass?

MAMA:
I didn't break the first one. You did.

LOLA:
I did not.

MAMA:
You did so.

LOLA:
Mama, don't say that. Your memory is bad enough without me having to sit here and belabor the point. You only think I broke the glass but you don't remember. Your mind is not the blazin' beacon it used to be. You don't even remember your own age.

MAMA:
I do so. I'm eighty-seven.

LOLA:
No, you're not. You're eighty-eight. I told you that yesterday and you forgot already.

MAMA:
I'm eighty-eight?

LOLA:
Yes, mama. On your last birthday, you was eighty-eight.

MAMA:
Where did that year go?

48

LOLA:
You see what I mean. You don't remember. No, it was you that broke the glass.

MAMA [*adrift*]:
That fly is still there.

LOLA [*smugly*]:
It's still there, but it's dead.

MAMA:
It doesn't look dead to me.

LOLA:
Maybe it's just squirmin' a little. [*Swatting the railing.*] There. That should do it. Dirty old fly. What use are they anyway. The Lord must have a reason but I don't know what it is…what reason there is for anything. The whole world has gone crazy, or seems to be goin' that way.

MAMA:
You know what I wish, Lola.

LOLA:
Maddy Finks is back in the crazy farm. They haven't found a net strong enough to hold her down. She's eighty-six. She's younger that you are, mama.

MAMA:
I wish I had a blue ribbon.

LOLA:
She broke glasses, too. She broke everything—good china—a vase that was in the family for three generations. She broke that, too. It was

49

blue sugarplum, like you can't even buy nowadays. What do you want a blue ribbon for?

[*LOLA is ignored by MAMA who assumes a vaguely aloof pose.*]

Mama?

[*A pause while MAMA fidgets with the arm of the rocker.*]

I said, what do want a blue ribbon for?

[*MAMA starts rocking. LOLA turns away.*]

You don't want a blue ribbon.

[*Another pause. MAMA continues rocking.*]

You only think you want a blue ribbon.

MAMA [*expressing hurt*]:
I don't have a blue ribbon.

LOLA:
I know that.

MAMA:
It would be nice to have a blue ribbon.

LOLA:
I'll get you one on your next birthday—if you don't pester me. I don't like to be pestered. Life is too short for that. That fly isn't dead looking' yet. [*She swats the railing again. While inspecting the swatter for the dead fly:*] She claims she was getting messages in her hair curlers.

MAMA:
Who?

LOLA [*shaking the fly loose*]:
Maddy Finks. Then she was captured by space people, with the big ears and wires comin' out of their heads that took her to Mars or some place.

MAMA:
To Mars?

LOLA:
I think it was Mars. I know it was on the other side of China. She said they stuck pins in her, too, like the Chinese do, with their needles. And then she flew off to Mars.

MARS:
Flyin' always scared me. I think I'd rather stay on the ground.

LOLA:
Well, she didn't actually fly. That was only in her head. That's why she's back in the crazy farm. She's crazy, mama. You don't go to Mars and come back again and not be crazy.

[*MAMA resumes her rocking.*]

I kinda thought she was slippin' when she papered the hen house with Easter grass. But when she came to church with her dress on backwards—and no shoes—well, I knew something wasn't right. That's what time does to you, mama. It affects the brain.

MAMA:
I still say you broke that glass.

LOLA:
Now let's not start that again, mama.

MAMA:
Because I know you broke it.

LOLA:
Alright, I broke the glass. Are you happy?…I said, does that make you happy?

MAMA:
My tooth hurts.

LOLA:
Oh, shush on your old tooth. I told you a hundred times you don't have any. Don't get weird on me, mama. I have enough on my mind tryin' to cope with the craziness that is all around us. [*Lowering her glasses.*] That is *not* Mr. Peabody. That is somebody else. He must still be at the grange.

MAMA:
Mr. Peabody must be at the grange.

LOLA:
That's what I said—if you'd listen.

MAMA [*after a pause; numbly*]:
Mrs. Peabody is dead.

LOLA:
I know that.

MAMA:
She died that summer we went to Davidson.

_____

LOLA [*with genuine surprise*]:
That's right, mama. She did. It was that same summer.

MAMA:
When it was so cold.

LOLA [*still straining to see*]:
I wonder. I just wonder who that could be.

MAMA:
That was a cold summer.

LOLA [*distracted*]:
Yes, it was, mama.

MAMA:
It was a *real* cold summer.

LOLA:
She was crazy, too, you know. Not real crazy, just medium crazy. She died from eating too many pills, that's what they said.

MAMA:
What did they say that for?

LOLA:
Because that's what she died of. [*More craning.*] I wonder if Mr. Peabody knows.

MAMA:
That she died?

LOLA:
Who that is in his house. It could be a burglar. Then it might be one of

his kinfolk. If we had a phone I could call. But then, if it's a burglar he probably wouldn't answer the phone anyway. No, I don't think it's a burglar.

MAMA:
It's still sticking.

LOLA:
What is?

MAMA:
My chair. It must be another piece of glass.

LOLA:
Another piece? It can't be.

MAMA [*picking up the glass object*]:
That's what it looks like. It's green though.

LOLA:
Green? We never had any green glass. [*Taking the object from mama.*] My lord, it is green. And it shines, too, in the dark. Isn't that something. [*Placing the object on the railing.*] See if there's any more pieces down there.

MAMA [*ignoring LOLA; focusing on the object*]:
I don't know if there is or not.

LOLA:
Well, you won't know if you don't look.

MAMA:
It glows in the dark.

LOLA:
That's what I just said. Lord, have mercy! You keep repeating things like you don't ever listen. You should know, that's a sign of old age— when you repeat things.

MAMA [*on auto replay*]:
When you repeat things.

LOLA:
That's right. Keep that up and you'll wind up like Maddy Finks. You wouldn't want that to happen.

MAMA:
I sure wouldn't want to be like her.

LOLA:
And I wouldn't blame you.

MAMA:
She lapsed into chewin' tobacco, you know.

LOLA:
No, I didn't know that.

MAMA:
Made her own cough syrup, too. Used to tone up on that every Saturday night.

LOLA [*smugly*]:
That must be what affected her brain.

MAMA:
Now you say she's back in the crazy farm?

55

LOLA:
Chained to a rabbit pen, that's what I'm told.

MAMA [*looking over the side of the rocker, dimly preoccupied with the search*]:
Must've been a real trip she was on.

LOLA:
It was a trip alright—in her head. Claimed they just scooped her up from the ground like a bale of alfalfa.

MAMA:
Who?

LOLA:
The space people—the ones with the funny ears and the wires pokin' out of their heads. What's more, she said the heat was so great, it turned everything to glass...*green* glass, I think she said. [*Peering out.*] That *is* a funny lookin' man over there. Can't figure out what he's doin'—just pokes around like he's lookin' for something. Kind of weird, isn't it, mama—the feelin' you get sometimes that something isn't right?

MAMA:
I don't feel anything.

LOLA:
Well, you wouldn't with your numbness. Maybe it's just craziness. So much of it goin' around. We think too much, that's what it is. The Lord didn't mean for us to think. He does that for us.

MAMA [*incredulously*]:
He does?

56

MY, BUT WASN'T THAT A COLD SUMMER!

LOLA:
It's in the Good Book, you know, that there will be craziness and more craziness. And that's when it comes—the Day of Judgment—when we all go to our Maker. That's something to think about.

MAMA:
The Lord doesn't want us to think you said.

LOLA:
Well, some things He does. You don't see any more glass down there?

MAMA [*pressing down on the rocker*]:
I don't feel anything.

LOLA:
I know that. I asked if you see anything.

MAMA:
I see a light overhead.

LOLA:
That's the moon, mama.

MAMA:
It doesn't look like the moon to me.

LOLA:
It does look kind of weird, now that you mention it. Must be something in the atmosphere. Rain, maybe. I did notice the air has gotten so close of a sudden. Did you notice that, mama? Like a body could rise up and float.

MAMA:
It was never in me to fly.

57

LOLA:
I didn't say 'fly.' I said 'float'—like in a balloon.

MAMA:
I feel fluffy a bit.

LOLA:
That's what I mean. There's something in the air.

MAMA:
It was that lemon cream pie we had tonight. You made it so fluffy.

LOLA:
I'm not talkin' that kind of fluff. It's a feelin' you get sometimes, like a fizz, you know…

MAMA:
You mean like a seltzer tablet?

LOLA [*uncharacteristically exuberant*]:
I mean like a giant bubble that just floats into space.

MAMA [*shaking her head*]:
I never felt that way…except once, when I was an angel bird.

LOLA:
You were what?

MAMA [*with gestures*]:
In school, when I was an itty-bitty bird and flapped my wings and flew over the Maypole.

LOLA:
Well, you better think about flyin' again, mama, 'cause there's something strange happenin' here. That man at Peabody's, he's comin' this way.

MAMA:
You mean the one with the big ears and the spoke comin' out of his head?

LOLA:
Well, I wouldn't call it a spoke exactly.

MAMA:
And his eyes shiny green like glass.

LOLA:
You noticed that, too?

MAMA:
And his gums a'clackin' like a loony bird.

LOLA:
I detect it more as a beepin' sound.

MAMA:
It'd be the first loony bird I know that beeped.

LOLA:
It boggles the mind what it could be.

MAMA:
Must be somebody from out of town.

LOLA [*with growing alarm*]:
I wasn't gonna say anything, mama, but since you noticed, I do believe with all the truth that is in me that we're bein' invaded by space people.

MAMA:
You mean like in the funny papers?

LOLA [*letting the magazine unroll. It is recognizable as a space-age scandal sheet*]:
I should've known right off, with the moon gettin' bigger and all, and the glass poppin' up on the floor—

MAMA:
And the floor poppin' up from the ground—

LOLA [*echoing MAMA*]:
And the floor poppin' up from the ground—Oh, my lord, it is! We're movin', mama. The ground is movin' out from under us.

MAMA:
That's what I said, you dumb thing.

LOLA:
We're risin' like a hot air balloon, that's what we're doin'!

MAMA:
I told you that pie was too fluffy.

LOLA:
Oh, damn you and that pie!

MAMA:
Well, it *was* too fluffy.

LOLA:
I don't make fluffy pies!

MAMA:
Then why are we leavin' the ground?

LOLA:
How should I know. We're just doin' it, that's all.

MAMA:
If you'd told me ahead a'time, I could've brought my toenail clipper.

LOLA:
Well, I didn't *know* ahead a'time!

MAMA:
My shawl, too. You left that on the cedar chest.

LOLA:
I asked you *nine* times if you wanted it.

MAMA [*looking down over the side of the chair*]:
There goes Mr. Peabody's house. It sure looks different from the topside. [*While looking away.*] Wonder where it is we're headin'?

LOLA [*at the railing, a hint of suppressed panic*]:
Lord only knows. It could be a mile or two and then it just might be to the end of the universe.

MAMA:
Is that further than Davidson?

LOLA:
You might ask Maddy Finks. She'd know.

61

MAMA:
She's back in the crazy farm.

LOLA:
That's what I mean.

MAMA [*after a pause*]:
She's never been to Davidson.

LOLA:
No, mama.

MAMA [*following another pause*]:
Been to Mars though.

LOLA [*smugly*]:
That's what she claims.

MAMA [*following a 3rd pause*]:
Wonder what it's like there in Mars.

LOLA [*back at her chair, dusting the seat with the magazine*]:
Oh, I imagine it's cold. It's a good bit from the sun, you know.
[*Swatting the railing with the magazine.*] That damn fly isn't dead yet.

MAMA:
As cold as that summer in Davidson?

LOLA [*resuming her seat*]:
Oh, I don't think it's *that* cold. I can't imagine anything being that
cold.

MAMA:
That was a cold summer.

62

MY, BUT WASN'T THAT A COLD SUMMER!

LOLA [*removing a hair curler*]:
That was a *real* cold summer. And so late! My lord! I thought it would never come, with the temperature down in the 40's all summer long, and the frost just huggin' the ground…

[*The lights dim to black at LOLA brings the hair curler to her ear.*]

Beyond the Gas

CHARACTERS

GEORGE, *an obsessive-compulsive*

EVELYN, *his obsessive-compulsive wife*

Beyond the Gas

SCENE: *The living room of GEORGE and EVELYN. They are seated several feet apart with a small table down front and center. GEORGE, a shirt on his lap, is threading a needle, or trying to. EVEYLN is examining a light bulb through a magnifying glass.*

A carton of light bulbs and a spool of thread are on the table, also a lamp minus its shade. A wall mirror is located down left.

There is a twenty-second pause.

EVELYN:
I suppose one of us should say something. The poor dears, they'll be bored silly before we get started.

GEORGE:
Started?

EVELYN:
This is a dramatic, dear. We're on the stage.

GEORGE [*looking up*]:
Oh?

EVELYN:
And I'm supposed to say good plays aren't being written anymore.

GEORGE:
I thought I was supposed to say that line.

EVELYN:
Well, it doesn't matter who says it. The fact is, it's true. Good plays simply aren't being written anymore. Why is, dear? Why aren't good plays being written anymore?

GEORGE:
Well, they're too repetitious for one thing. They keep saying the same thing over and over. It's monotonous.

EVEYLN:
That's true.

GEORGE:
And who really cares. They don't come to grips with real problems.

EVEYLN:
They lack bearing, isn't that what you mean, George? It's a question of bearing.

GEORGE:
Exactly.

EVEYLN:
Human experience is one thing. People live and breathe and have feelings, but with bearing.

GEORGE:
You can relate.

EVELYN [*at the table, unscrewing a light bulb*]:
Like having a tooth pulled. Or spilling catsup. A universal experience.

GEORGE [*still trying to thread the needle*]:
Evelyn, I'm trying to see.

EVELYN:
An emotion that you can share—have empathy for—to empathize. Is that a word, George—empathize?

GEORGE:
You just changed that light bulb two minutes ago.

EVELYN:
Why don't they write about us. We're people. We have emotions and things.

GEORGE:
I don't know why you have to keep changing light bulbs.

EVELYN:
Maybe we're not interesting. Maybe we should *do* something.

GEORGE:
That would be clever.

EVELYN:
I mean something extraordinary—that would set us apart.

GEORGE [*trying to rethread; mildly sarcastic*]:
It's this absence of stress. It's killed our motivation.

EVELYN [*studying a light bulb she has removed from the carton*]:
It would have to be big—bigger than we are. But what? What's bigger than we are? Name something, George.

GEORGE [*raising the needle above his head to see better*]:
Evelyn, please.

EVELYN:
The world is just full of problems—enormous ones, too. Oh, the challenge is there alright, when you think of it. My goodness, our very survival is at stake. [*Referring to the bulb.*] Isn't it pretty, George?

GEORGE:
Damn it all, if I have to put on more spit—

EVELYN:
Well, isn't it?

GEORGE:
It's getting so limp now it just droops.

EVELYN:
The bulb, George—isn't it pretty?

GEORGE:
They all look the same to me.

EVELYN:
But this one is different, George. It's a different one altogether.

[*GEORGE gives up for the moment.*]

You'd think that would be an incentive to write a good play.

GEORGE:
A light bulb.

EVELYN:
No, silly. Survival. The fact that we might not survive.

69

GEORGE [*clenching the thread between his teeth...*]:
Maybe they don't care about survival. [*... and breaking it.*]

EVELYN:
Oh, they care alright. Everyone cares.

GEORGE [*moistening the thread*]:
It sounds boring.

EVELYN:
Maybe to you, George. I happen to consider survival very important... Well, isn't it?

GEORGE [*aiming the thread at the eye of the needle, but missing*]:
I suppose if you're into mat weaving or class reunions.

EVELYN:
You're bitter, George, because you can't thread a needle.

GEORGE:
Anyway, it's too academic. Either you survive or you don't. What can we do about climate change? Or the H-bomb? Not to mention the pain of psoriasis. What about that, Evelyn?

EVELYN:
What about it?

GEORGE:
There's no cure for that either.

EVYLYN:
Really, George.

GEORGE:
That should make a good play. A morality play.

EVELYN [*back to her light bulbs; undaunted*]:
Geraldine has acidosis.

GEORGE [*half-expecting the unexpected*]:
That figures.

EVELYN:
No, George. She really has acidosis. I meant to tell you before but I forgot. She swallows air.

GEORGE:
I suppose if there's no other way of getting it.

EVELYN:
It's a shame, too. She keeps getting the hiccoughs, isn't that something? The doctor says she's hyperventilated, whatever that means.

GEORGE:
It means she's a windbag.

EVELYN:
No, it doesn't. It's nerves. She's always been high strung, you know that.

GEORGE:
Maybe she would make a good play. We can't do anything about these enormous problems, so we ventilate.

EVELYN:
Geraldine? Don't be silly.

GEORGE:
Well, we don't just ventilate. We hyperventilate. But it doesn't end there. We keep on ventilating until finally...

EVEYLN:
We get acidosis.

GEORGE:
No. The hiccoughs. Then we're in trouble.

EVELYN:
With that plot I'd say the *play* was in trouble. What happens then?

GEORGE:
Nothing happens. You just learn to live with the hiccoughs.

EVELYN [*back at the lamp, switching bulbs*]:
I don't think that's so smashing.

GEORGE:
My god, Evelyn, why do you keep doing that?

EVEYLN:
Why, why, why! How should I know? I just like to, that's all.

GEORGE:
I think you're peculiar.

EVELYN:
What about you and your silly old buttons? I don't begrudge you that. If you want to sew every night until midnight—

GEORGE:
I wouldn't have to if you ever learned how.

EVELYN:
They're not even loose.

GEORGE:
I say that they are.

EVELYN:
In your mind they're loose. But they're not really loose.

GEORGE:
Evelyn, please.

EVELYN:
I've gone over them, George. I've tested them—every time I get you a new shirt, I test them. Honestly, I do.

GEORGE:
I'd rather be sure.

EVELYN:
They're good shirts.

GEORGE [*sharply*]:
I never said they *weren't* good shirts.

EVELYN:
Then stop making fun of my light bulbs.

GEORGE:
You should be analyzed.

EVELYN:
Maybe we both should.

GEORGE:
I don't believe in it.

EVELYN:
But it's alright for me. Oh, I don't know, George. I search myself trying
to figure you out.

GEORGE:
I find you rather puzzling myself.

EVELYN:
That's what I mean, George. There's more to us than meets the eye, no
matter what the writers think. [*Back to switching bulbs.*] I mean, here
we are in space and time—in the middle of nowhere. Think of it,
George. Isn't it awesome? Nowhere. I mean we don't even know where
we are.

GEORGE:
I don't know what's so awesome about that.

EVELYN:
But we can think of it. We have the power to look at ourselves and to
think 'what does it mean, George?'

GEORGE [*attempting to rethread the needle*]:
You're in the light, Evelyn.

EVELYN:
Oh, I get so desperate sometimes when I think of the whys and
wherefores of things, don't you?

GEORGE [*dismissively*]:
Yes, I do.

BEYOND THE GAS

EVELYN:
How it all came about—existence and everything. It makes you wonder.

GEORGE:
It all goes back to roast duck and boiled potatoes.

EVELYN:
What does?

GEORGE:
Creation. That's how it began.

EVELYN:
I don't believe it.

GEORGE:
It's quite simple. About thirteen billion years ago the world was a lot of hot gas, like it is today. It was writhing and twisting and boiling until it lost so much steam that it solidified.

EVELYN:
What happened to the roast duck, George?

GEORGE:
There wasn't any roast duck.

EVELYN:
I thought you said there was.

GEORGE:
That's how quick it all happened—in the time it takes to roast a duck and boil potatoes.

EVELYN:
You didn't say that, George.

GEORGE:
Of course, it's only a theory.

EVELYN:
And that's how it all began—hot gas and everything?

GEORGE:
That should make a good play.

EVELYN:
It's silly, George. I mean, there you are—it's hot gas. So what? It doesn't say anything.

GEORGE:
You're right. There has to be something beyond the gas. But what? What is beyond the gas?

EVELYN:
I wish I knew, George.

GEORGE:
It doesn't get at the supreme enigma.

EVELYN:
No, it doesn't.

GEORGE [*facetiously*]:
It should go to the heart of the matter, like 'what is beyond the gas?' What does it mean—not as an exercise in cosmic abstractions—but it terms of the human spirit. Answer that one, Evelyn. How do we fit into whatever it is that we're in? Think, think, Evelyn.

76

EVELYN:
Oh, I knew it, George. We can be profound. We can look at the night sky and say "What does it all mean?" Isn't that wonderful—that we can do that?

GEORGE:
It's absolutely wonderful.

EVEYLN:
It shows that we're reaching. That we're destined for something higher.

GEORGE:
You mean the stars and all that?

EVELYN:
And beyond. That should make a good play.

GEORGE:
People reaching?

EVELYN:
Well, wouldn't it, George?

GEORGE:
It's too up in the air.

EVELYN:
Oh, that's funny, George.

GEORGE:
Okay, so you're reaching. Who's going to pay money to see that?

EVELYN:
I hate to say this, George, but you have the mind of a midget.

GEORGE:
I agree.

EVELYN:
You'll never be anything more than you are.

GEORGE:
Oh, for Pete's sake, stop that infernal switching.

EVELYN:
And you could be, George, if you had the ambition.

GEORGE:
I do have the ambition.

EVELYN:
Then why aren't you ahead?

GEORGE:
Because I'm inept, that's why. I was born to be a midget. You can't be more than you are.

EVELYN:
You can try.

GEORGE:
I do try. I try all the time. I reach, Evelyn.

EVELYN:
But not high enough, George.

GEORGE:
I go to old Gimlet Eyes and I say, "Old Gimlet Eyes, I looked at the stars last night and I want to tell you, they're something. The next time

when you're not having a board meeting or a department audit I want you to look at the night sky and ask yourself 'what does it all mean?' What does it all mean, Gimlet Eyes? That's what you want—action! Don't be a midget all your life. Do something big. Be more than you are. Well, I'm not big, Evelyn. [*Almost in tears.*] I'm not big.

EVELYN [*soothingly*]:
You are big, George, if you say that you are.

GEORGE:
Oh, bosh!

EVELYN:
George, I'm telling you, you are. Your are, you are!

GEORGE:
Damn it, it's come loose. The button is loose. It's all your fault.

EVELYN [*undaunted*]:
You *are* big.

GEORGE:
Will you shutup. I'm trying to do something here and you keep frustrating me.

EVELYN:
George, you're upset.

GEORGE:
I'm going to take that goddamn bulb and break it.

[*He grabs the lamp, smashing the bulb on the table.*]

EVELYN [*quietly aghast*]:
George, you broke my bulb.

GEORGE:
You're goddamn right I did.

EVELYN:
You smashed it.

GEORGE [*mimicking*]:
It's a pretty bulb. Isn't it pretty, Evelyn—all these nice little pieces?

EVELYN [*snatching his shirt from the chair*]:
I can play games too, George.

GEORGE:
Give me that shirt.

EVELYN:
All these pretty white buttons. Aren't they pretty, George?

[*She rips the buttons from the shirt and throws them to the floor.*]

Here, chickie, chick-chick-chick!   Here, chickie, chick-chick-chick!
It's feeding time.

GEORGE [*franticly picking up the buttons*]:
Evelyn, you're going too far.

EVELYN:
All you think about is buttons.

GEORGE:
I'm warning you, Evelyn.

___

EVELYN [*still tearing buttons*]:
You could be important, reach for the stars, but all you do is sit around and sew buttons. Why don't you reach?

GEORGE [*at EVELYN'S throat*]:
I am reaching.

EVELYN:
George, you're choking me.

GEORGE:
All my life I've tried to build something decent and true but you have to destroy, destroy!

EVELYN:
George, I can't breathe!

GEORGE:
You think it's trivial, sewing buttons. Well, buttons are very important to me, I want you to know that.

EVELYN:
George, you're killing me.

GEORGE:
I want to be profound, to be more than I am, but you won't let me. You have claw and peck away and make me feel like a midget. Well, I'm not a midget. I might say that I am just to be agreeable, but I'm not.

EVELYN:
You're big, George.

GEORGE:
You're damn right I'm big. I can outthread you anytime, remember that, Evelyn.

EVELYN:
I've never denied it, George.

GEORGE:
You've never admitted it either.

EVELYN:
You're a wonderful threader, George. Now let go of me, please.

GEORGE:
Then say it like you mean it.

EVELYN:
George, you're pinching a nerve!

GEORGE:
Promise me that much. Will you do it, Evelyn?

EVELYN:
Oh, I do, George. I promise.

GEORGE:
Cross your heart—solemnly?

EVELYN:
As soon as I'm able, George.

GEORGE:
Hope to die?

EVELYN:
George, for heaven's sake, let me surrender!

[*He releases her. She goes to the mirror and massages her neck. A slight pause.*]

EVELYN:
I do wish you would cut your nails.

GEORGE:
I wasn't planning on using them.

EVELYN [*more massaging*]:
It's the only neck I've got, George.

GEORGE [*retrieving the shirt*]:
Yeah? Well, look what you did to my shirt—no buttons.

EVELYN:
I'm sorry. I'll get you a new one—with zippers.

GEORGE:
That's fine, because I'm having the house rewired for kerosene.

EVELYN [*a mood softening*]:
No, really. I had planned on getting you one anyway. The collar is frayed.

GEORGE [*responding in kind*]:
So it is. I hadn't noticed.

EVELYN [*picking up the half-empty spool*]:
You'll need more thread. The buttons are never as tight as they should be.

GEORGE:
They just don't make shirts like they used to. Why is it, Evelyn? Why don't they make shirts like they used to?

EVELYN:
It's the stitching, mostly. Oh, the fabric is there alright. It's better than ever.

GEORGE:
That's true.

EVELYN:
Broadcloth, polyester—and cotton. Don't forget that. Where would we be without cotton?

GEORGE:
It's all in the thread, how they stitch it.

EVELYN:
What *is* the world coming to?

GEORGE:
I wish I knew.

EVELYN:
They don't make anything like they used to.

GEORGE:
Except the bombs. They're better.

EVELYN:
Here's your thimble, George.

GEORGE:
Uranium, plutonium, hydrogen. And neutron, don't forget neutron. They're the best.

84

EVELYN:
Is that how it ends, George? The world? In a tizzy of smoke?

GEORGE:
Not really. It's more like a fizzle. It runs out of gas.

EVELYN [*removing a bulb from its carton*]:
Like a bad play, you mean? It doesn't go anywhere.

GEORGE:
Of course, it's only a theory.

EVELYN:
But we go on, don't we, George? Whatever the scene?

GEORGE [*attempting to rethread the needle*]:
That we do.

EVELYN [*twirling the light bulb in her hand*]:
Forever spinning…

GEORGE [*missing the eye*]:
Oh, damn, damn, damn!

EVELYN:
And cursing…

GEORGE:
And threading needles.

[*The stage dims to black.*]

You *Will* Tell Rodney

CHARACTERS

NARRATOR

DAVID

EMILY

SCENE: *The Hamptons*

You *Will* Tell Rodney

SCENE: *A spot focuses on the NARRATOR on an otherwise darkened stage. A maudlin musical rendering serves as background.*

NARRATOR:
Once upon a time there was a great American institution called The Soap Opera. For many long and troubled years it pulled at the heartstrings of a nation, producing a medley of tears and jeers and a curious bittersweet longing for the more aseptic life.

For thirty years it reigned supreme—and then one day it ended—its bleached remains quietly buried in the cliché-washed catacombs of Madison Avenue.

If you can bear with us we're going to dig up this corpse for a few short moments and show you how it might have looked with some of the bleach removed.

[*The NARRATOR exits. Lights up on EMILY seated at a table devouring a cob of corn and facing DAVID who is standing.*]

DAVID:
My dear Emily, how radiant you look tonight.

EMILY:
Oh, David, I can't tell you what happiness it is, just to be near you, to know that you're back

DAVID:
You missed me, I hope.

EMILY:
I was simply empty without you. It's not very exciting here in Bellhampton. I mean it's not the best place in the world for a—*premature* widow.

DAVID:
Why don't you come to New York?

EMILY:
I told you—

DAVID:
But Rodney will be out of school in another month.

EMILY:
It's not only that, David. He's only a boy. He wouldn't understand.

DAVID:
Have you told him—about us, I mean?

EMILY:
I tried to, David. Only yesterday, when he was repairing his motorcycle. He looked so much like Anthony—the same eyes, so full of wonder.

DAVID:
He's not a boy anymore, Emily.

EMILY [*biting savagely into her cob*]:
I'm so weak, David. Soft, I suppose. It was never in me to hurt anyone.

DAVID [*relieving her of the cob, putting it on a separate plate*]:
You're hurting yourself, Emily. You can't go on denying the fact. The truth is important. Whatever else is involved, the truth *is* important.

EMILY:
Oh, I hope so. I do, David. But I'm not sure. If it was only the boy.

DAVID:
Yes, if it was only the boy.

EMILY:
But it's Elvira, too. Will she ever forgive us. Poor Elvira. To think she's been so trusting—even today, after all this bitterness.

DAVID:
I tried to explain, Emily, the best way I could. I—I told her, of course.

EMILY:
You told Elvira?

DAVID [*offhandedly*]:
About you killing Anthony. She was utterly credulous.

EMILY:
Credulous? Elvira? She'll go to the police.

DAVID:
Yes, I thought of that afterwards. So I persuaded her not to. Gently, of course—the only way I could.

EMILY:
You killed Elvira?

DAVID:
You *will* tell Rodney—about us, I mean?

[*Blackout.*]

Orange Pekoe on the Rocks

CHARACTERS

A BOY

A GIRL

SCENE: *A patio at tea time*

Orange Pekoe on the Rocks

SCENE: *BOY and GIRL sit, with teacups in hand, facing a small table with decorative teapot and a dish containing a single sugar cube.*

BOY:
Nice day.

GIRL:
Couldn't be nicer.

BOY:
Wonderful tea.

GIRL:
Glad you like it.

BOY [*awkwardly*]:
Lovely pot.

GIRL [*coolly*]:
Thanks a lot. [*A slight pause. She reaches for the teapot.*] Another cup?

BOY:
If you please.

GIRL:
Sugar cube?

BOY:
Just a lump.

ORANGE PEKOE ON THE ROCKS

GIRL [*aiming the cube*]:
Oh, dear me!

BOY:
You missed the tea.

GIRL [*with a fumbling gesture*]:
Yes. Yes, I did, didn't I. I'm so embarrassed.

BOY:
I wonder where it went.

GIRL:
It was my last lump, too. The one I've been saving.

BOY:
Really?

GIRL:
It must have dropped on the floor. Disgusting, isn't it.

BOY:
It's only a sugar cube.

GIRL:
I've never done that before. I feel so dirty about it.

BOY:
It's perfectly normal.

GIRL:
It's not very nice.

BOY:
Some of the nicest people I know have dropped their sugar cubes.

GIRL:
I wish I could believe that.

BOY:
I've done it myself.

GIRL:
Have you really?

BOY [*nodding*]:
Twice.

GIRL:
Oh, god, I'm so relieved. Thank you for telling me.

BOY:
You're quite welcome.

GIRL:
I was afraid I was the only one. [*Settling back.*] I feel much better now.

BOY:
I'm glad you're feeling better.

GIRL [*after a pause; carefully*]:
When did you drop your sugar cube—the first time, I mean?

BOY:
I'd rather not say—if you don't mind.

GIRL:
I understand.

BOY:
It's quite painful.

GIRL:
I can imagine.

BOY:
You don't mind my not telling you?

GIRL:
No, of course not.

BOY:
Thank you.

GIRL [*after another pause*]:
I'd offer you another lump but I don't have any. That was my last lump.

BOY:
Yes, you told me.

GIRL:
I could put it under the faucet, I suppose.

BOY:
It would disintegrate under water. It does that, you know—sugar.

GIRL:
Well, I wouldn't run it too long.

BOY:
Do you think you could get all the dirt out?

GIRL:
I don't honestly know. It's one of those 'iffy' things.

BOY:
We could try, I suppose.

Girl:
Why don't we.

BOY:
You won't tell anyone?

GIRL:
No, of course not.

BOY:
I wouldn't want people to think I was eating—well—dirty sugar.

GIRL:
Heaven forbid!

BOY:
I have to think of my image. You do understand?

GIRL:
I know what you mean. I'm in this thing, too, remember.

BOY:
Yes, you are.

GIRL:
We both are.

BOY:
It seems so diabolic.

ORANGE PEKOE ON THE ROCKS

GIRL:
I wonder if it has anything to do with original sin?

BOY:
I hope so.

GIRL:
So do I.

BOY:
I've always wanted to live dangerously. Secretly, of course.

GIRL:
Same here.

BOY:
Should we?

GIRL:
It's your lump.

BOY:
It's your faucet.

GIRL:
Oh, god, I feel so ashamed.

BOY:
Please don't.

GIRL:
You won't think less of me?

BOY [*clasping her hand passionately*]:
I will always love you, you know that. Nothing will ever change.

GIRL:
You won't hate me?

BOY:
I said 'I love you.'

GIRL:
You can't love me and not hate me. They go together, you know.

BOY:
I'm sorry. I forgot you were being analyzed.

GIRL:
You will hate me then—just a little?

BOY:
Oh, god, I'll try.

GIRL:
You know, I never realized you were such a dog.

BOY:
Funny. I was thinking the same about you.

GIRL:
I always thought you were a nice person.

BOY:
Did you really? I always knew you were a fake.

GIRL:
I guess we're both pretty rotten—in a nice way, of course. I mean there's nothing gross about us.

BOY:
Heaven forbid.

GIRL:
I wouldn't want to be gross.

BOY:
Nor would I.

GIRL:
I want to be nice.

BOY:
Do you really?

GIRL [*rises, cup in hand*]:
Yes, I do. Because the important thing is to be nice.

BOY [*joining her, cup in hand*]:
I agree.

GIRL [*moving downstage; reciting, with a beat*]:
I mean, who cares what's under the skin,
so long as you've got that exterior grin,
the important thing is to be nice.

BOY [*joining her downstage*]:
Who cares.

GIRL:
Who cares?

99

BOY [*reciting*]:
Who cares if the soul is made of ice,
when a few well-chosen words will always suffice,
so be nice; the important things is to be nice.

GIRL:
Now take people for instance. There are nice people and there are un-
nice people…

BOY:
And there's the other ninety-nine-and-nine-tenths percent of the
population…

GIRL:
Like us for instance…

BOY:
Who only seem like they're nice…

GIRL:
But who are, in fact, quite the opposite.

[*A music tag as both turn their backs to the house. When they face the
house again their hair is disheveled, their voice and demeanor take
on a toughness.*]

GIRL:
Another cup?

BOY:
Orange Pekoe on the rocks, baby. Hold the sugar.

GIRL [*obliging*]:
You got it.

BOY:
Pour yourself a swig. I don't like drinking alone.

GIRL:
Sure thing. [*She pours herself a cup.*] What do we do now?

BOY:
We get smashed, what else?

[*They click cups and sip.*]

GIRL:
What got you started—on this kick, I mean?

BOY:
Pimples mostly. I used to have pimples.

GIRL:
I had some pretty hard bumps myself.

BOY·
I should've let them alone, but I squeezed them.

GIRL:
I know how it is. I had blackheads.

BOY:
No kiddin'?

GIRL:
I should've squeezed 'em but I let 'em alone. [*A pause.*] Another cup?

BOY:
Slam it.

[*She pours.*]

My old lady drank Liptons.

GIRL:
The poor kid.

BOY:
The old man was hooked on Salada.

GIRL:
Yeah, I know. The broken home bit.

BOY:
They were always yellin'—pullin' the strings on each others tea bag. It was crazy. Every night they were sloshin' tea bags until finally…

GIRL:
Go on.

BOY:
They got separate garbage cans.

GIRL:
Oh, god!

BOY:
So I left. I felt with my pimples, it was more than I could take.

GIRL:
My old man was an addict. Aspirin. My old lady, too. She took the buffered. He liked it straight. They would race to see who could get to the bloodstream first. The tension was killing. What was a simple headache would turn into migraine. Regular aspirin was useless. No

102

kick. They would go to Anacin, Monocet Compound, Emperin, and finally…*ibuprofen*!

BOY:
Geez.

GIRL:
The place reeked with salicylic acid. You'd go painless just breathing the stuff. I'd say, "Ma, ain't you gonna make supper? I'm hungry." And she'd pass the aspirin bottle.

BOY:
That's tough.

GIRL:
From then on it was downhill—SMOOSH—all the way. I tried to look back, search out what had gone wrong but it was useless. So here I am—debauched at thirteen.

BOY:
I'm fourteen. I guess you got debauched before I did.

GIRL:
If we could only start over.

BOY:
Yeah.

GIRL:
Life would be different.

BOY:
No pimples.

GIRL:
No blackheads.

BOTH:
Tea bags or aspirin.

GIRL:
Let's try.

BOY:
I'm game.

GIRL:
Another cup.

BOY:
If you please.

GIRL:
Sugar cube?

BOY:
Just a lump.

GIRL:
Oh, dear me, I missed the tea.

BOY:
You didn't miss the tea. There wasn't any more sugar. Who're you kidding?

GIRL:
Now wait a minute.

BOY:
What are you—senile? 'Oh, dear me, I missed the tea!' when it's been sitting right there [*Pointing.*] on the floor all along—filthy!

GIRL:
Get out!

BOY:
You must think I'm stupid.

GIRL:
It's the last tea party you'll be invited to.

GIRL:
Yeah? Then give me back my teapot.

[*She obliges.*]

And my cups.

[*She obliges.*]

And my saucers.

[*She obliges.*]

What about the sugar cube?

GIRL:
What about it?

BOY:
It was my sugar cube. You borrowed it.

105

GIRL [*picking it up from floor, she drops it in a cup*]:
Yuk!

BOY:
So…what about next time?

GIRL:
Next time?

BOY:
At my house. Orange Pekoe on the rocks, baby. With lemon!

GIRL [*turning tough*]:
I gottcha.

BOY:
See ya then.

[*He goes off with the serving pieces. Music tag and blackout.*]

Poor Pigeon

CHARACTERS

CEDRIC

PANHANDLER

COUNTER MAN

LADY CUSTOMER

PATROLMAN

JUDGE

BANK OFFICER

CEDRIC'S WIFE

PSYCHIATRIST

SCENE: *A New York City park*

Poor Pigeon

SCENE: *A New York City park. CEDRIC, a timorous bank clerk, is feeding the pigeons from a paper bag. The action takes place outside the curtain.*

CEDRIC:
I'm a happy man. That's right. I'm a happy man because in thirty days—another month—I'm going to retire on a big, fat wonderful pension that a big, fat wonderful bank is awarding me for a lifetime of big, fat wonderful service. And when I get that big, fat wonderful pension, me and my big, fat wonderful wife are going to take a once-in-a-lifetime trip to the South Seas which we are both eagerly anticipating and that's why I'm a happy man.

Right now I'm feeding the pid-ge-ons which I always do on my lunch hour and which has been a custom of mine for over thirty years.

[A PANHANDLER appears. He is a supercilious type, dressed in the tattered remains of top hat and tails.]

PANHANDLER:
I beg your pardon, Sir. Could you spare a poor supplicant a pittance for a cup of coffee? Only a pittance, I ask no more.

[CEDRIC reaches into his pocket and gives the PANHANDLER A coin.]

Thank you, Sir. You *are* a jelly bean!

[*The PANHANDLER starts off, then stops after a step or two.*]

PANHANDLER:
Oh, Sir.

[*There is a slight pause before he gets CEDRIC'S attention.*]

This is a trifle. I asked for only a pittance.

[*CEDRIC points to his pocket, then shrugs.*]

You don't have a pittance? Well, good heavens, man, why didn't you say so? There's a drugstore on the corner. We can get some change there.

[*He returns the coin, then takes CEDRIC by the arm, escorting him to stage center, as the curtain opens to a drugstore setting.*]

[*To the COUNTER MAN.*] Oh, Sir, would you be a goodie and give this man change for a trifle.

[*The COUNTER MAN, who has been wiping the counter, dismisses him with a wave of the hand.*]

Oh, come now. You have to have change—a big store like this.

COUNTER MAN:
I only got change for customers.

PANHANDDLER:
How do you like that! He only has change for customers—the dirty chauvinist. Wait. I, have it. I'll be a customer. That way he'll have to give us change.

CEDRIC:
That's a very good idea.

PANHANDLER [*aside*]:
Oh, he talks, too. How clever.

CEDRIC:
Then I can get my change and start back to the office.

PANHANDLER [*with dripping sarcasm*]:
Oh, Sir. Would you slosh your way to the urn and get me a nice hot cup of coffee.

[*The COUNTER MAN exits.*]

CEDRIC:
That way I won't be late.

PANHANDLER:
Oh, I'm terribly sorry. I'm keeping you. You were going somewhere?

CEDRIC:
Well, I'm on my lunch hour.

PANHANDLER [*happily surprised*]:
Oh, you work?

CEDRIC [*smiling modestly*]:
In a bank.

COUNTER MAN [*reentering*]:
Here's your coffee.

CEDRIC:
It'll be thirty years next month.

PANHANDLER [*feigning wonder*]:
Thirty years!

CEDRIC:
Then I get a pension.

COUNTER MAN [*to CEDRIC*]:
That'll be two pittance.

CEDRIC:
We're planning on a long vacation, the Mrs. And I.

PANHANDLER [*to the COUNTER MAN, indignantly*]:
Two pittance?!

CEDRIC:
To the South Seas.

PANHANDLER:
What is this, highway robbery? The idea! Two pittance for a cup of coffee. [*To CEDRIC.*] Don't you give him more than a one.

CEDRIC:
All I've got is a trifle.

COUNTER MAN [*to CEDRIC*]:
Com'on, buddy, you're wasting my time.

PANHANDLER [*to CEDRIC*]:
You give him that trifle and I'll throw this coffee in your face.

CEDRIC:
I've got to give him something.

111

PANHANDLER:
Good heavens, man, doesn't principle mean anything?

COUNTER MAN [*grabbing CEDRIC from across the counter*]:
Okay, buddy, let's have it. I ain't got all day.

PANHANDLER [*intervening*]:
Just a minute, Sir. Who, do you think you're pushing around?

COUNTER MAN:
You keep out of this.

PANHANDLER [*to CEDRIC*]:
He's already made one pittance profit. Now he wants more. Well, he won't get it. Tell him that.

COUNTER MAN [*to CEDRIC*]:
Are you calling me a cheat?

CEDRIC:
I didn't say anything.

PANHANDLER:
Yes!

CEDRIC:
I mean 'no.' I mean, I didn't say that. He did.

COUNTER MAN [*drawing CEDRIC closer*]:
You miserable creep. I aughta bust every bone in your body!

PANHANDLER:
I'd like to see you try. [*To CEDRIC.*] Tell him that.

COUNTER MAN:
Who threw the coffee in my face?!

CEDRIC:
I-I-I--

COUNTER MAN:
YOU?!

CEDRIC:
I mean, no, he did. I mean somebody did.

COUNTER MAN [*buckling up his fist*]:
Alright, buddy, you asked for it.

[*A right uppercut and CEDRIC falls to the floor, his head colliding with a vending machine. A LADY CUSTOMER, who has been sitting nearby, starts up.*]

LADY CUSTOMER:
Police! Police! Police!

[*The PANHANDLER runs off. The COUNTER MAN leaps over the counter and pins CEDRIC to the floor. A patrolman enters waving a nightstick.*]

PATROLMAN:
Okay, break it up. [*To CEDRIC.*] You, there. What's your name?

COUNTER MAN:
He wouldn't pay his check, officer.

PATROLMAN:
One of them guys, eh?

COUNTER MAN:
He called me a cheat and threw coffee in my face.

CEDRIC:
It's not true, officer. I was more than willing—

COUNTER MAN [*almost in tears*]:
But the most dastardly thing of all, he broke the hot, chocolate machine.

PATROLMAN:
No!

COUNTER MAN:
I swear, officer. He smashed it—with his own head.

CEDRIC [*incredulously*]:
I smashed it?

PATROLMAN:
What are you, a maniac?

LADY CUSTOMER [*coming forward*]:
It was his head, officer. I saw it.

CEDRIC [*getting up*]:
Of course, it was my head. He pushed me.

PATROLMAN:
A likely story.

CEDRIC:
I was standing right here buying this man a cup of coffee—

___

PATROLMAN:
What man?

CEDRIC [*looking around, startled*]:
Well, I mean there was a man here…someplace…be-because I saw him, officer.

PATROLMAN [*grabbing CEDRIC'S arm, starting off*]:
You can tell that to the judge.

[*A JUDGE pops up from behind the counter (now serving as a trial bench) pounding his gavel. The PATROLMAN goes off.*]

JUDGE [*in a monotone*]:
Solemnly swear the truth, the whole truth and nothing but the truth, so help you God. Step down.

CEDRIC [*raising his right hand*]:
I do. I do, your honor.

JUDGE:
Do what?

CEDRIC:
Solemnly swear.

JUDGE:
Don't get cute with me. This is a court of law.

CEDRIC:
I understand that, Sir. I mean your honor.

JUDGE:
And you broke it in three different places.

CEDRIC:
But I didn't, Sir. It was a mistake.

JUDGE:
What do you mean, a mistake? You heard the charges.

CEDRIC:
But I'm contesting them, Sir.

JUDGE:
Contesting—authentic charges? What are you, a troublemaker?

CEDRIC:
But I'm innocent, Sir.

JUDGE:
You admit you didn't pay the check.

CEDRIC:
I wanted to, Sir.

JUDGE:
You wanted to, but you didn't.

CEDRIC:
No, you honor.

JUDGE:
And the coffee you didn't pay for, you threw in his face, didn't you?

CEDRIC:
No, I didn't.

116

JUDGE:
Don't lie to me. There's two witnesses who said you did. You don't have any witnesses.

CEDRIC:
No, your honor.

JUDGE:
I suppose you're going to tell me you didn't break the hot chocolate machine?

CEDRIC:
Well, I broke it—

JUDGE:
Of course, you broke it. It was your head, wasn't it?

CEDRIC:
It was accidental.

JUDGE:
Accidental, my eye. It was premeditated savagery. I want you to know the law doesn't countenance that kind of behavior.

CEDRIC:
No, your honor.

JUDGE:
That'll be two hundred smackers.

CEDRIC:
Two hundred smackers?!

JUDGE:
You heard me. Pay the clerk.

CEDRIC:
But, Sir—your honor—all I have is a trifle.

JUDGE [*lowering the gavel*]:
Thirty days in the workhouse.

CEDRIC:
Thirty days?

JUDGE:
See if we can't work off some of that exuberance of yours.

CEDRIC:
But, Sir—

JUDGE:
Don't 'sir' me.

CEDRIC:
I'm on my lunch hours.

JUDGE:
You'll eat with the other prisoners. Next case, please.

[*The BANK OFFICER appears, left, on a phone, as the court scenes dims out.*]

BANK OFFICER:
I'm sorry, Cedric, but thirty days on a lunch hour. Tsk, tsk, tsk. We just can't permit that at Mercenary Trust and Savings. Why, before you know it everyone and his brother would be going around breaking hot chocolate machines and where would we be then, I ask you, Mercenary—I mean Cedric? And now with a prison record and all that, I'm just afraid it's going to be very embarrassing for us to—well, put

you back on the payroll. I know you've been a faithful and conscientious servant and that you were due for a nice fat pension in another month, but now with all this scandal and everything—well, it just breaks my heart to see a good man like you go down the drain. Of course, you understand we can't recommend you for another banking position with your—er—record. Yes, I know, Cedric, you age will make it difficult for you to start over and that your dear wife, bless her heart, was counting desperately on that once-in-a-lifetime trip to the South Seas…

[*Cross fade from BANK OFFICER to CEDRIC'S WIFE, stage right, on a phone.*]

CEDRIC'S WIFE:
Of course, I believe you, Cedric. Only this morning I said, when you left the house, I said, "I bet he gets thirty days for breaking a hot chocolate machine." You drip. What do you think I am—stupid? I don't know why I put up with you. If it wasn't for that big, fat pension and the once-in-a-lifetime trip to the South Seas…What do you mean, your fired? Well, that's the last straw, I tell you. There's no food in the house. The rent's due tomorrow. Bloomingdale's want their furniture back. What am I going to do? I can't pay them. There's 32 cents in the coffee can. That's my reward for putting up with you all these miserable years. Well, I'm leaving. You can live out your stagnant, apathetic life alone, do you hear? Our marriage is finished, kaput, aus gespeiled, you-you-you hot chocolate machine breaker!

[*She slams the receiver. A jail psychiatrist appears, stage center, with stethoscope, clipboard and mallet. He is examining CEDRIC, seated cross-legged on a stool. Dim out on CEDRIC'S WIFE.*]

PSYCHIATRIST:
Say 'ah.'

[*There is an uneasy pause. He hits CEDRIC'S knee with the mallet.*]

CEDRIC:
Aaaaah!

PSYCHIATRIST:
That'll teach you. There's not going to be any schizophrenics in my prison.

CEDRIC:
No, Sir.

PSYCHIATRIST:
Try those withdrawal symptoms on me, by god, and I'll show you. Too much running away from things. We should face our destiny with a bold front.

CEDRIC:
Yes, Sir.

PSYCHIATRIST:
Why don't you face your destiny with a bold front? Don't you like the world?

CEDRIC:
Oh, I like the world alright.

PSYCHIATRIST:
Then why don't you react?

CEDRIC:
I do react.

PSYCHIATRIST [*illustrating with clipboard*]:
React, my eye! Look at your electroencephalogram. There isn't a trace of activity. If it wasn't for that low voltage of slow 7-per-second waves I saw yesterday I'd say you were dead.

CEDRIC:
Yes, Sir.

PSYCHIATRIST:
We can't discharge dead people. What would the newspapers say? They're just aching for us to make a mistake. How do you think they sell, newspapers?

CEDRIC:
I don't know, Sir.

PSYCHIATRIST:
Maybe we should sent you to the mortuary.

CEDRIC:
Whatever you say, Sir.

PSYCHIATRIST:
Your thirty days are up. We can't rehabilitate you.

CEDRIC:
No, Sir.

PSYCHIATRIST:
Have you ever tried panhandling?

CEDRIC:
No, Sir.

PSYCHIATRIST:
Well, you better learn because that's the only way you'll ever get by.

CEDRIC:
Yes, Sir.

PSYCHIATRIST [*offering him a coin*]:
Here, take this. There's a shuttle leaving in ten minutes. It'll get you to skid row. [*Taking a folder from his pocket while showing him out.*] And a manual on how to put the bite on pedestrians. But for Pete's sake, don't mumble.

CEDRIC [*examining the coin*]:
But, Sir—

PSYCHIATRIST:
I said not to mumble.

CEDRIC [*stops, looking back*]:
This is a trifle. Shuttle service is only a pittance.

PSYCHIATRIST [*dismissively*]:
Well, it just so happens, Cedric, I don't have a pittance.

CEDRIC [*with uncharacteristic boldness*]:
Well, good heavens, man, why didn't you say so? There's a drug store on the corner. We can get some change there.

[*He grabs the PSYCHIATRIST by the arm and exits. The COUNTER MAN makes a sudden appearance in the background.*]

Oh, Sir, would you be a goodie and give this man change for a trifle…

[*Blackout.*]

122

Centrifuge

an anti-play featuring action
that goes nowhere

CHARACTERS

GEORGE
GRETCH, *his wife*
EMIL, *a guest*
HUGO, *another guest*

Centrifuge

SCENE: *EMIL, GEORGE, GRETCH and HUGO are seated Buddha-like on floor cushions, stage l. to r., respectively. Their arrangement is roughly semicircular with a larger space separating EMIL from the others.*

At rise, EMIL is gazing into a mirror, GEORGE is pondering a paper flower, HUGO is filling a shot glass from a pint of Pussywillow bourbon, GRETCH is shuffling a deck of cards. A jar of peanut butter and a woman's purse are on the floor next to GRETCH.

EMIL:
Sixty drams is not a lot of something for a Dalmatian marshmallow, is it Newburg? I mean Hubert. Oh, dash it all, I'm bleeding! My penchant for palliation is purple dye-cast and there's no point in being intelligible.

GEORGE [*focusing on the flower*]:
Emil, you are right. It's a case of miasmic miscegenation and we'll just have to keep flubbing at the mustard, irrespective.

HUGO [*with raised glass*]:
Hotshot! Bullyboy! Schlupping glug on a Persian rug is what I call smug. Pussywillow anyone? [*He drinks up.*]

GRETCH [*shuffling cards*]:
On a cash basis? I don't think so. Mangy emotions are murder on my hypodermic, so cut it. [*She places the deck down by HUGO who cuts it.*]

124

HUGO:
Pig suet, anyone?

EMIL:
No, person to person.

GEORGE:
I'll take it.

[*GEORGE takes the mirror from EMIL and puts the flower in his hair. GRETCH is dealing.*]

HUGO:
The point we're really making is that if you actually try to communicate with your fellow man, you're hopelessly hung on a syntactical rung. In plain gibberish, your corpus-dyslexus is showing. In this age of "awesome" and "cool" it is imperative that we uphold the "doctrine of universal meaningless," which is to say, speak in tongues that are so arcane—

GEORGE:
So convoluted...

GRETCH:
And so egregiously alien to the human mind as to defy both logic and comprehension.

HUGO:
Hear, hear!

[*GEORGE puts the mirror down and picks up his cards.*]

HUGO:
The pivotal thing—I say pivotal—is that we exercise our psychical

125

apparatus on the subjective lever, that is to say, work out our psychoneurosis, group therapy and all, because it's fun.

EMIL:
It's kicky.

HUGO:
Right you are. The idea, you see, is to keep talking but not really say anything.

GRETCH:
Talk, talk, talk, talk.

EMIL:
But don't be comprehensible.

HUGO:
No action, no plot. Just talk. Oedipus and Hamlet and Blanche DuBois were all monologists.

GRETCH:
And they had fun.

HUGO:
Of course, they were a tad canoodled. Only a fool would want to know who he really is.

GRETCH:
Rudolph Valentino had a ulcer.

HUGO:
With dialogue like that it's so easy to cut. You don't have to worry about continuity.

EMIL:
So easy on the knuckles, too. No grease, no splatter. No unsightly leftovers, completely bloodless.

GRETCH:
My cousin Harry used to snort bonbons.

HUGO:
That's cool. I like that.

EMIL:
Like bracketing your iron oxide on a facetious tulip.

GEORGE:
It's all a matter of anti-relativity.

EMIL:
God is torture.

HUGO:
I pass.

GEORGE:
Tennis anyone?

EMIL:
Don't be unreasonable.

HUGO:
And so it goes. Don't—I beg of you—try to be logical or you'll miss the whole point. Just relax and enjoy us. Because we're fun, and we enjoy ourselves. How about that?

GRETCH:
George, I've got a feeling.

GEORGE:
Don't lead. I told you not to lead.

GRETCH:
I'm not leading. All I said is "I've got a feeling."

GEORGE:
Then suppress it. There's nothing so cheap as a resolved feeling.

EMIL:
If she's got a feeling, George, for heaven's sake, let her have it.

GEORGE:
All it does is excite emotion and conflict. You want them to start listening?

GRETCH:
I'm sorry, George.

HUGO:
You can tell me, but whisper it. [*She whispers something in his ear.*] She doesn't know who she is.

GEORGE:
Is that all?

GRETCH:
I don't, George.

EMIL:
I was a rug once. [*A slight pause while he waits for a reaction.*] A rug.

GRETCH:
I don't, George. Honestly.

HUGO:
What kind of rug were you.

EMIL:
It was Omar Khayyamish, really—with accents of Ohio Chemical.

HUGO:
How extraordinary.

EMIL:
Yes, it had lotus blossoms entwining an oxygen tank.

GEORGE [*reciting*]:
"I sent my soul through the invisible..."

EMIL:
I knew what I was. I could adjust.

GEORGE:
"For some letter of this afterlife to spell..."

EMIL:
I didn't like what I was but at least I was spared the uncertainty of not knowing.

GEORGE:
"And bye and bye my soul returned to me..."

HUGO:
Was it a flash of intuition or a moment of self-revelation?

EMIL:
It was more like a flash.

GEORGE:
"And said—"

GRETCH:
George, I can't go on this way.

GEORGE [*with signs of growing anger*]:
"I am both—"

GRETCH:
I mean it, George.

GEORGE:
"I am both—"

HUGO:
Who's got a cigarette?

[*GRETCH obliges with a pack from her purse.*]

GEORGE:
I will not be interrupted!

EMIL:
It was terrific, really. All your life you think 'well, here I am, a human being, that you're alive and have feelings and isn't it wonderful...'

GEORGE;
Damn it all, let me finish. "I am both heaven and hell."

EMIL:
And then it happens. You wake up one day and you say, "My god. My god, I'm a rug!"

130

HUGO [*dousing the cigarette*]:
I hate filters.

GRETCH:
I was floor lamp once.

GEORGE:
I told you not to build on it.

GRETCH:
I'm sorry.

EMIL:
Can't we be pointless.

HUGO:
I always light the wrong end.

GRETCH:
Let's kill somebody.

GEORGE:
You're feeling again.

GRETCH:
No, I'm bored. Can't we start a war or something?

GEORGE:
Wars are immoral.

GRETCH:
Yes, but they break the monotony.

HUGO:
I have a better idea. Why don't we make peace more offensive.

EMIL:
That's all very well, Hugo. But how?

HUGO:
We could love people to death, clobber them with olive branches. They'd be so mushed up, they wouldn't know what hit them.

GRETCH [*gleefully*]:
They'd hate us.

HUGO:
Precisely.

EMIL:
Sounds delightfully putrid.

GEORGE:
Like kissing Hitler.

GRETCH:
I don't think I'd be up to kissing Hitler.

HUGO:
I wouldn't have to be Hitler. It could be Adolph Schneck.

GEORGE:
Who's he?

HUGO:
I don't know. I never heard of him.

GRETCH:
That's funny. Neither have I. He must be quite famous.

EMIL:
I remember him. He was a midget philosopher from Stoke Poges. He used to paint lemons and sell them as Easter eggs.

HUGO:
My word, I thought that was the Prince of Wales.

EMIL:
So many people were eating boiled lemons for breakfast he was knighted by the packaging industry.

GRETCH:
Sounds like the perfect fraud.

HUGO:
We'd certainly want to kiss *him*.

EMIL:
We can't do that either. He's dead.

HUGO:
I'm sorry to hear that.

EMIL:
He was assassinated by a Mau Mau who thought he was a chicken.

GRETCH:
Adolph Schneck was a chicken?

EMIL:
No, no. The Mau Mau thought *he* was a chicken.

HUGO:
I can see why he was offended.

EMIL:
The curious thing was he did lay a few eggs. What he resented was the fact that he had to sell them as lemons.

HUGO:
My word.

GEORGE:
We could kiss *him*, I suppose.

GRETCH:
I'm not sure I'd want to kiss someone who laid an egg and called it a lemon. I think I'd rather be bored.

HUGO:
May I say something.

GEORGE:
Don't.

HUGO:
Adolph Schneck was a cad.

HUGO:
Alright, I won't.

GEORGE:
You just did.

GRETCH:
I didn't hear anything.

GEORGE:
You weren't listening.

EMIL:
I heard it.

GRETCH:
What did he say?

EMIL:
He said you weren't listening.

GRETCH:
Oh, I heard that too.

GEORGE:
How do we get out of this?

GRETCH:
I have a solution. Let's resolve not to solve anything.

HUGO:
I wish I thought of that.

GRETCH:
If you don't have any solutions, then all you have left is problems.

HUGO:
Oh, I say, that is a Fig Newton.

GRETCH:
And if all we have left are problems, we're that much closer to chaos.

HUGO [*calling out*]:
Mr. Chairman!

GRETCH:
I'm not the chairman.

HUGO:
I didn't say you were.

GRETCH:
I'm a devoted Methodist.

HUGO:
The thesis that you can solve problems by not solving them is a non sequitur.

GRETCH:
Before that I was a philodendron.

HUGO:
What you are proposing is, in effect, planned chaos.

GEORGE:
I was a rhododendron.

HUGO:
Well, you can't plan chaos. It must come from the heart.

GRETCH [*to EMIL*]:
What were you?

EMIL:
I was a rug once.

HUGO:
It's well known that chaos by its very definition cannot be organized or it ceases to exist as chaos.

GRETCH:
You're against chaos.

HUGO:
I'm not against chaos. I simply reject organized chaos as a workable hypothesis.

GEORGE:
Sounds pornographic to me.

GRETCH:
He's probably never even met a hypothesis, much less a workable one.

EMIL:
I used to know a parenthesis.

HUGO:
What was she like?

EMIL:
Standoffish—a real bracket.

GEORGE:
Really, gentlemen, we're making too much progress.

GRETCH:
I had the same feeling.

HUGO:
She's feeling again.

GEORGE:
I move that we accept his rejection of planned chaos as a workable hypothesis so we can get on to more inconsequential matters.

GRETCH:
Very well, but only on the condition that it's unconditional.

GEORGE:
The motion, as I understand it, is that we proceed on the condition that we unconditionally accept his rejection.

EMIL:
I use a stick shift myself.

GRETCH:
Are we voting?

HUGO:
I'm not sure I understand the issue.

GEORGE:
Then it's agreed.

GRETCH:
Those in favor of organized chaos signify by not doing anything.

HUGO:
How will we know if we're not doing anything?

GRETCH:
It's easy. We'll pretend we're marshmallows.

EMIL:
I get it. We'll just pretend we don't know if we're not doing anything. That way we won't actually know anything if we do it.

GRETCH:
Exactly.

EMIL:
On second thought, I'm not sure I want to commit myself.

GEORGE:
As a voting marshmallow I think we should recess.

GRETCH:
What on earth for?

GEORGE:
We need more time to get confused.

HUGO:
Good. Then I don't have to second the motion. I was afraid we might reach a decision. [*Raising his brandy bottle.*] Pussywillow, anyone?

EMIL:
I would but I'm preaching.

[*GRETCH screams for no apparent reason.*]

HUGO:
What was that?

EMIL:
I didn't hear anything.

HUGO:
Somebody screamed.

GRETCH:
It must be those raspberry seeds. They keep getting stuck.

GEORGE:
I thought you were eating strawberries.

GRETCH:
From a peanut butter jar?

GEORGE:
Maybe it was a peanut.

GRETCH:
No, George. It was a raspberry seed. I've eaten enough peanut butter to know a raspberry seed when I choke on it. Here's your purse.

GEORGE [*removing a mirror and powder puff from the purse*]:
It's not even logical.

GRETCH:
What is?

GEORGE [*patting his face with the puff*]:
Raspberry seeds in a peanut butter jar. What's the world coming to?

GRETCH:
I wish I knew, George. I wish I knew…

[*Blackout.*]

Invitation to a Russian Wake

CHARACTERS

COUNTESS IVANOVITCH

SOBALONYA KARPINSKI

UNDERTAKER

GYPSY JOE

VASNA

NIKOLAI

COMMISSAR LITVINOV

THE SPIRIT OF NODNIK

SCENE: *The foyer of a Moscow funeral parlor*

Invitation to a Russian Wake

SCENE: *The foyer of a Moscow funeral parlor, sometime in autumn.*

The air of solemnity is quickly established through the use of potted ferns and subdued lighting. A few folding chairs grace the area and come into use for brief periods. Upstage, left, is a lectern containing a register for names of people attending the wake, and, up center, a curtained entrance leading to the main chapel. A door to the street and adjoining window are located right, along with a bust of Lenin used as a hat rack.

At rise, COUNTESS IVANOVITCH, a smartly dressed woman of pre-Revolution vintage, enters from the chapel, followed by SOBALONYA KARPINSKI, an elderly gray-haired lady whose face is partly hidden by a handkerchief. Both women are dressed for mourning. Overture to "Prince Igor" carries under the opening lines.

COUNTESS IVANOVITCH:
I can't believe it. Yesterday I saw him, just yesterday. He came over to see the new Zug. Dmitri got a new Zug, did I tell you?

SOBALONYA KARPINSKI:
No, Countess Ivanovitch.

COUNTESS IVANOVITCH:
Such a card he was—cutting up like a hooligan!

SOBALONYA KARPINSKI [*pressing the handkerchief to her nose*]:
He was a good boy.

COUNTESS IVANOVITCH [*at the register, flipping pages*]:
He was a wonderful boy, Sobalonya Karpinski. You couldn't ask for a better son if you had the whole world for a picking.

SOBALONYA KARPINSKI:
You sign, Countess Ivanovitch, so that you will be in the Book of Remembrance.

COUTESS IVANOVITCH [*with pencil in hand, pointing it at S.K.*]:
Not one enemy did he have in all of Moscow. He was well regarded, Sobalonya Karpinski—very well. [*She pats her arm sympathetically.*] And so young—in the prime of his life. It's a shame that he should be laid out at such a young age. He would have made a fine husband.

[*SOBALONYA KARPINSKI emits a long mournful cry, followed by hideous, uncontrollable sobs.*]

Six girls, of the most gorgeous girls—pleading with him to get married. He was that popular. Dmitri will tell you. Dmitri will tell you.

SOBALONYA KARPINSKI [*echolng weurily*].
Dmitri will tell me.

COUNTESS IVANOVITCH:
I wanted so much for Dmitri to see him, to see what a nice job they did. They did a nice job, Sobalonya Karpinski. It's a joy to know there's a least one man in Moscow who takes pride in his work.

SOBALONYA KARPINSKI:
You will be busy without Nodnik.

COUNTESS IVANOVITCH:
Without Nodnik we are practically helpless. I need someone in Kharkov on Tuesday and with the garter exhibit just one week away

143

and not one single agent east of Omsk—it's discouraging. If poor Nodnik was here it would be both places for Nodnik, he was such a blitz.

SOBALONYA KARPINSKI:
He was a good salesman.

COUNTESS IVANOVITCH [*more pointing with the pencil*]:
He was the best salesman we ever had. Sold more garters on the black market than all the others combined. [*Signing the register.*] He was a remarkable man, Sobalonya Karpinski. In many ways. In many ways he was a remarkable man.

SOBALONYA KARPINSKI:
You sign Dmitri Ivanovitch so that he, too, will be in the Book of Remembrance.

COUNTESS IVANOVITCH [*obliging*]:
Three nights ago at the Bolshoi, when he walked into his box at the Bolshoi—five ballerinas swallowed their chewing gum. They had to stop the music, it was such a distraction…Maybe he was right, not to comply—to live like he did. It is not for us to judge.

SOBALONYA KARPINSKI:
No, Countess Ivanovitch.

COUNTESS IVANOVITCH [*moving away from the lectern*]:
So he burned the candle at both ends. So maybe he had a reason. Everything has a reason. You've got a reason. I've got a reason. Moscow has a reason. Or why would it be? Why would we be, Sobalonya Karpinski?

SOBALONYA KARPINSKI [*glancing towards the window*]:
Commissar Litvinov should be here soon.

COUNTESS IVANOVITCH:
And the Commissar. He has a reason. What is his reason, Sobalonya Karpinski?

SOBALONYA KARPINSKI [*half-muttering*]:
I don't know, I don't know.

COUNTESS IVANOVITCH [*overlapping*]:
Why is he any better than Nodnik. Commissar Litvinov could never sell garters. He couldn't even sell toothpaste. I remember him when he was in Minsk. He wasn't such a lily either. He had his weaknesses.

[*The offstage sound of a car coming to a halt.*]

SOBALONYA KARPINSKI:
He is coming now, I think.

COUNTESS IVANOVITCH [*at the window, looking out*]:
It's alright, Sobalonya Karpinski. It's only the hearse.

SOBALONYA KARPINSKI [*starting to break*].
I tried to be good to him, like a mother—to teach him the good life.

COUNTESS IVANOVITCH [*putting her arm around S.K.*]:
Of course, you did, Sobalonya Karpinski.

SOBALONYA KARPINSKI:
But he never listened. "Mama," he would say, "it's my life. Let me live it." Forty-two years. Such a young boy—just out of confinement.

[*UNDERTAKER and florist GYPSY JOE enter at stage right. They are dressed appropriately in black with sealskin caps which they remove immediately upon entering. GYPSY JOE carries two empty flower baskets. More cries from SOBALONYA KARPINSKI which escalate*

145

into more uncontrollable sobs. The UNDERTAKER goes to S.K. and rests his hand on hers gently.]

UNDERTAKER:
Be brave, Sobalonya Karpinski. In some ways he is more lucky than we.

[*SOBALONYA KARPINSKI catches her breath, then more sobbing. The UNDERTAKER exits into chapel.*]

COUNTESS IVANOVITCH:
You can be grateful that you still have Nikolai and Vasna.

SOBALONYA KARPINSKI [*between gulps; incredulously*]:
Nikolai and Vasna!

COUNTESS IVANOVITCH:
That you are not alone in the world like the widow Trotsky.

[*The UNDERTAKER returns from chapel and goes to GYPSY JOE.*]

UNDERTAKER [*sotto-voiced*]:
The Commissar isn't here—Commissar Litvinov.

GYPSY JOE [*muttering*]:
Oy, yoi yoi.

UNDERTAKER:
My right arm I would give if he was on time once. The dead can wait while he fiddles.

[*Two voices are heard from inside the chapel. They draw nearer.*]

COUNTESS IVANOVITCH [*touching the UNDERTAKER'S wrist*]:
You did a good job, believe me. He never looked better.

UNDERTAKER [*ignoring the COUNTESS; to GYPSY JOE*]:
When he's on a case I use twice the formaldehyde.

COUNTESS IVANOVITCH:
So natural he looks—like he was sleeping.

[*VASNA and brother NIKOLAI enter from the chapel. VASNA has a handkerchief pressed to her nose. NIKOLAI is pouring over a newspaper.*]

VASNA [*while entering*]:
What's keeping Commissar Litvinov?

COUNTESS IVANOVITCH [*to UNDERTAKER*]:
As unnatural as it was for him to be sleeping.

NIKOLAI [*to VASNA*]:
Maybe he forgot.

VASNA:
Forgot? For twenty rubles Commissar Litvinov would not forget the devil.

[*A series of gasps from SOBALONYA KARPINSKI.*]

COUNTESS IVANOVITCH:
He is only sleeping, Sobalonya Karpinski. For awhile. For a little while.

[*A loud sustained cry, followed by more uncontrollable sobbing. The UNDERTAKER and GYPSY JOE return to the chapel.*]

147

NIKOLAI:
Mama, please. If he's sleeping, let him sleep. The poor boy, he needs it.

VASNA [*viewing the register*]:
It's the most sleep he's got in his whole life. It's a pleasure, believe me.

SOBALONYA KARPINSKI:
A pleasure?!

NIKOLAI:
At least we know he's out of trouble, mama.

SOBALONYA KARPINSKI:
He was a good boy.

VASNA:
He was a profligate, mama—a capitalist beast. He was no good to nobody.

SOBALONYA KARPINSKI [*proudly*]:
He sold more garters on the black market than anyone. Countess Ivanovitch will tell you.

VASNA:
Ten thousand a year for the last seventeen years and not a kopeck did he leave. What good is garters, mama, if he can't pay for his own funeral? [*Leaving the lectern.*] You should know that, Countess Ivanovitch. Thirty-five suits of imported silk, a 12-cylinder Juggernaut and a chewing gum wrapper in his pocket when he died. He wasn't a profligate, mama? What was he—Albert Schweitzer? A humanitarian?!

SOBALONYA KARPINSKI:
He was good to me.

VASNA:
A two-pound box of Nikita's Crunchies—every year for her birthday! That was his contribution. [*To S.K.*] What happened to the ten thousand rubles? I'll tell you what happened.

SOBALONYA KARPINSKI:
Vasna, please.

VASNA:
Wine, women and song! That was his creed. And executions! You should know about the executions. When he came out to Minsk—I was with him that time.   Four hundred rubles he wagered on two commissars. I had to give him gas money back to Moscow. Did he ever offer to pay it back—when Gregory was in the hospital and I had to work nights as a bench girl in a munitions factory? He never once mentioned the gas money.

SOBALONYA KARPINSKI:
So why bring it up now?

VASNA [*undaunted*]:
Who got the Juggernaut, mama?

SOBALONYA KARPINSKI:
It's not important who got the Juggernaut.

VASNA:
Natasha Smolenski got the Juggernaut. Natasha Smolenski—a chorus girl at the Bolshoi! What did we get, mama? Grief! That's all we ever got was grief.

[*More sobs from SOBALONA KARPINSKI. The COUNTESS embraces her sympathetically.*]

149

COUNTESS IVANOVITCH:
Now, now, Sobalonya Karpinski. It could be a communist just as easy.

SOBALONYA KARPINSKI:
A heart attack. I don't understand. Four generations on both sides and not one heart attack. Treason and frostbite and deficiency syndrome but not one heart attack.

COUNTESS IVANOVITCH:
If it was God's will—

VASNA:
If it was God's will, Papa would have stopped after Nikolai. He would have spared us that much anyway.

SOBALONYA KARPINSKI:
Commissar Litvinov will say something nice about Nodnik. You wait and see.

NIKOLAI:
Commissar Litvinov did not even know Nodnik.

COUNTESS IVANOVITCH [*to S.K.*]:
He was well regarded, very well.

VASNA:
How many people came to the wake, mama? How many?

SOBALONYA KARPINSKI:
What does it matter how many—

VASNA [*pointing*]:
Look at the register. Six people. Five chorus girls and a librarian. Not a respectable one in the bunch. That's the proof of his worth.

150

SOBALONYA KARPINSKI:
Countess Ivanovitch has come.

VASNA:
Countess Ivanovitch is his confidante. I'm talking about friends. People who go to a wake because they want to, not because they have to. When Natanya died—

SOBALONYA KARPINSKI:
Now we come to Natanya!

VASNA:
There was two hundred names in the register. With flowers—from every ball bearing plant in the city. And FOOD! I never saw so much corn meal and biscuits and hash. We had strength to grieve then. This time we can starve. That's how well he was regarded.

SOBALONYA KARPINSKI:
It was not all his fault.

VASNA [*producing a large pocket watch, eyeing it quickly*]:
If that Commissar Litvinov doesn't get here pretty soon—

SOBALONYA KARPINSKI:
He was just a young boy when Papa died.

VASNA:
It's thirty miles to the cemetery.

SOBALONYA KARPINSKI:
I had more pain when Nodnik was born, twice as much as I had with you, Nikolai.

VASNA:
It's way past New Rochellograd. They'll be closing the gates before we get there.

SOBALONYA KARPINSKI:
He grew up on the streets—with Muzhiks. There was no one to teach him.

VASNA:
The Muzhiks, mama! They should be the ones who should worry. It was their misfortune that he took to the streets.

[*GYPSY JOE enters from the chapel with a basket of flowers and goes to the door, right.*]

VASNA [*to GYPSY JOE*]:
You better take them all because it's gonna look pretty naked at the cemetery.

SOBALONYA KARPINSKI:
When I was alone, it was Nodnik who stayed. You went to Rostov and Minsk and Sevastopol. Moscow wasn't big enough for your plans.

[*GYPSY JOE exits.*]

VASNA [*to NICKOLAI*]:
Did you see the gardenias?

SOBALONYA KARPINSKI:
But Nodnik stayed—in my house!

VASNA:
I never saw such tired looking gardenias.

152

SOBALONYA KARPINSKI:
In my house he stayed!

VASNA:
The next time when somebody dies we're not using Gypsy Joe. Besides, I heard from Constantine Rubicoff that he goes through the graveyard like a vulture and steals all the baskets. The ground isn't even cold and he steals the baskets.

[*A long, shrill whistle, off.*]

VASNA [*jumping up, rechecking her watch*]:
My god, the factories are letting out! Where is Commissar Litvinov?

NIKOLAI:
Yes, where is the Commissar? Why must we always wait. It was the same with Natanya.

VASNA:
We'll give him five minutes. If he doesn't come in five minutes we'll fake the credentials ourselves. We won't need the Commissar.

SOBALONYA KARPINSKI:
What a thing to say!

VASNA:
We can't sit around all day waiting for the Commissar. It's nine hours to Minsk. That'll give us just enough time to punch in at the shale pit.

SOBALONYA KARPINSKI:
You wait for the Commissar. I'm going in.

[*SOBALONYA KARPINSKI exits to the chapel. VASNA, who has been pacing back and forth, stops by the window. NIKOLAI has crossed to the lectern.*]

153

NIKOLAI [*looking up from the register*]:
Natasha Smolenski isn't in the register.

VASNA:
Natasha Smolenski is too busy rounding up all the other suckers. She's got his Juggernaut. Why should she care.

NIKOLAI:
She is dancing tonight in "Swan Lake." There's a big splash in Pravda.

VASNA:
There'll be a bigger splash if she ever lets go of her two feet. She's got as much grace as a scarecrow.

NIKOLAI:
They are giving it special for the Minister of Ectoplasmic Consent and his delegation of Ukrainian Corn Shuckers. She will be riding the crest.

VASNA [*with expansive gestures*]:
What a mess that will be! I'm glad I'm not going.

COUNTESS IVANOVITCH [*to VASNA; with reverence*]:
When she dances tonight, she will be dancing for Nodnik.

VASNA:
Baloney, she will. She will be dancing for joy! And that Minister of Ectoplasmic Consent. She had her eyes on him since Odessa, when she was a guest at his dacha. That was a weekend, believe you me. Because I heard all about it from Constantine Rubicoff on Shaski Street and what a tramp she is. She's dancing for nobody but the top side of a ruble and there's not one minister left in the whole Secretariat that don't know it— [*Pointing towards the outdoor entrance.*] sitting right today, in the Secretariat!!!

154

[*COMMISSAR LITVINOV makes his appearance during VASNA'S tirade, but is unnoticed by her. By now, all but VASNA are facing the COMMISSAR, a short, solemn-faced man toting a portable phonograph.*]

NIKOLAI [*cautioning her*]:
Vasna.

VASNA [*still pointing, but looking in another direction*]:
The shameless beasts!

COUNTESS IVANOVITCH [*with reserve*]:
Commissar Litvinov.

[*VASNA smiles foolishly while others remain silent, half-expecting the COMMISSAR to respond. He pauses long enough to remove his cap and place it on the bust, then looks to NIKOLAI with a sadness that is plainly rehearsed.*]

THE COMMISSAR:
Where is the mama?

NIKOLAI:
She is inside, Commissar.

[*The UNDERTAKER reenters from the chapel. His presence is acknowledged immediately by the COMMISSAR.*]

THE COMMISSAR [*to UNDERTAKER*]:
Such a tragedy.

COUTESS IVANOVITCH [*to COMMISSAR*]:
He was well regarded. Very well.

THE COMMISSAR:
Tied up in traffic for two hours! What a tragedy!

UNDERTAKER:
The traffic is heavy?

THE COMMISSAR:
Heavy? It's impossible. It will be six hours to Rosemont.

VASNA:
Six hours?!

THE COMMISSAR:
They had an explosion at the Bureau of Ectoplasmic Consent. Hypodermic needles all over the street. Nine people dead—all of them Corn Shuckers. What a tragedy!

[*GYPSY JOE enters from the street.*]

GYPSY JOE [*to COMMISSAR; with outstretched arms*]:
Commissar Litvinov!

THE COMMISSAR [*with delight*]:
Gypsy Joe, you thief! [*They embrace.*] How is the flower business?

GYPSY JOE:
Stinking, Commissar. Absolutely stinking! There is no sentiment for the dead. Nowadays they are telling people to send money, they are so cheap. I have to use the same baskets twice to make a profit.

UNDERTAKER [*softly*]:
The mama, she is waiting for you, Commissar.

156

THE COMMISAR:
Quick. Give me the summary. The Book of Remembrance, where is it?

UNDERTAKER:
On the lectern, Commissar.

THE COMMISSAR [*passing the phonograph to the UNDERTAKER as he goes to the lectern*]:
I had the facts all written down so they could be stenciled and what did I do? I sent the whole business to the House of Machiavelli for a refill. They'll never believe it. [*Flipping a page.*] What is the name—Nodnik Karpinski? Age: forty-two, born in Moscow, died in Moscow. What killed him?

UNDERTAKER [*placing the phonograph on a chair*]:
What killed him?

THE COMMISSAR:
It doesn't say what killed him.

NIKOLAI [*to VASNA*]:
He wants to know what killed him.

VASNA:
Tell him life—too much of it!

UNDERTAKER [*slipping a record on the turntable*]:
A heart attack, Commissar.

THE COMMISSAR:
Haven't got too much time so can't give it the full treatment. Have another wake on Shaski Street. Constantine Rubicoff, you remember him?

GYPSY JOE:
Connie Rubicoff, the junk man?

THE COMMISSAR [*rips a page from the register, then crosses to the front door*]:
A profligate, that's all he was. A capitalist beast. Left is wife and six kids; took up with a fan dancer from Sevastopol. Positively worthless. [*Opens the door, looking out.*] Where is the body? I can't see a thing.

[*UNDERTAKER drops the needle to Schumann's "Spring Symphony", then discovers the COMMISSAR has meandered outdoors.*]

UNDERTAKER:
Commissar Litvinov.

THE COMMISSAR [*from the street*]:
Who's calling my name?

UNDERTAKER [*at the door, pointing towards the chapel*]:
The parlor is this way

THE COMMISSAR [*reentering*]:
I'll never make it. They quit serving at ten. [*Stops at the phonograph.*] For what is the music?

UNDERTAKER:
You don't want music?

THE COMMISSAR [*removing the record, then flipping it over*]:
I am sick of this misery and suffering. What I would give for a good gypsy funeral and a brass band. That was a feast! [*He puts the needle to a lusty Ukrainian folk dance, then whirls to stage center, in tempo.*]

COUNTESS IVANOVITCH [*clasping her hands, gleefully*]:
I can't believe it! I can't believe it!

[*The COMMISSAR moves gaily across the room, his movements gradually taking on the aspects of a dance, largely free style.*]

THE COMMISSAR [*sweeping the COUNTESS along*]:
Nine people dead. All of them Corn Shuckers. What a tragedy!

COUNTESS IVANOVITCH [*with delight*]:
That it's you, I can't believe it!

[*Their tempo increases as the music grows more vibrant. They circle the room in full sway. Others break a path, gathering in couples.*]

THE COMMISSAR [*shouting to UNDERTAKER from a distance*]:
How much time have we got?

UNDERTAKER [*shouting back*]:
Exactly twelve minutes, Commissar Litvinov.

[*Taking their cue from the COMMISSAR, the others quickly follow suit. First it is NIKOLAI and VASNA who fall in line, then, after some mutual misgivings, GYPSY JOE and the UNDERTAKER. The ensuing dialogue is projected over the music background.*]

THE COMMISSAR [*while passing the UNDERTAKER*]:
I'll give them the Muzhik, Dvorak and moan routine.

UNDERTAKER:
You can do that in twelve?

THE COMMISSAR:
I can do it in six.

UNDERTAKER:
That's a good routine, Commissar.

THE COMMISSAR:
The freckled-face boy in the streets of Moscow. It never fails. You get a reaction every time.

GYPSY JOE [*passing the COMMISSAR*]:
It's a sad one, the Muzhik, Dvorak and moan.

THE COMMISSAR:
Haven't given it in a month.

NIKOLAI:
He was just a boy, Commissar. Such a good boy.

VASNA:
Always remembered his mother.

THE COMMISSAR [*ignoring VASNA*]:
Tell me, Countess Ivanovitch, how is the black market these days?

COUNTESS IVANOVITCH:
Don't mention the market!

THE COMMISSAR [*giving the COUNTESS a whirl*]:
I hear that it's booming.

COUNTESS IVANOVITCH:
It's got me in a spin! What a spin I'm in!

GYPSY JOE [*to UNDERTAKER*]:
You're scuffing my shoes.

COUNTESS IVANOVITCH:
I need someone in Kharkov on Tuesday and with the garter exhibit just one week away—

THE COMMISSAR:
You lost a good man in Karpinski

COUNTESS IVANOVITCH:
And not one single agent east of Omsk.

THE COMMISSAR:
Forget about Omsk. You need a man down in Kharkov, let's face it.

COUTESS IVANOVITCH:
I'm tearing my hair out!

THE COMMISSAR:
I got just the man.

COUNTESS IVANOVITCH:
Who, Commissar Litvinov? Tell me who?

THE COMMISSAR [*with a glint*]:
ME, Countess Ivanovitch.

COUNTESS IVANOVITCH:
YOU?!

THE COMMISSAR:
It could be me.

[*NIKOLAI cuts in, dancing off with the COUNTESS. VASNA is left with the COMMISSAR who looks on, momentarily bewildered.*]

161

COUNTESS IVANOVITCH [*looking back, smiling but ominous*]:
It could be, but I'm not so sure.

THE COMMISSAR [*with mounting anguish*]:
It has to be!

COUNTESS IVANOVITCH [*gliding on with NIKOLAI*]:
I'm still not so sure.

THE COMMISSAR:
You don't understand, Countess Ivanovitch—

COUNTESS IVANOVITCH [*pointing towards the phonograph*]:
The music, it's too loud in my ear.

THE COMMISSAR [*pursuing the COUNTESS*]:
I wouldn't be doing this, but it's come to a point. I think you know what I mean.

COUNTESS IVANOVITCH:
I got a sneaking suspicion.

THE COMMISSAR [*upsetting a chair in his pursuit*]:
There hasn't been a purge in six months. I'm way under par. Last year I had my quota in June. Everything else was prerogatives. This year I have to buy what I can on the free market. [*Stepping over the chair.*] I'm only a Commissar of Parks; I'm not a Minister of Power. If production is off he can put on a swing shift. I can't tell people to drop dead.

COUNTESS IVANOVITCH [*shouting from across the room*]:
The question is: can you sell garters? It's not like it is on the outside. It's a buyers' market. If they don't like what you sell, they don't buy it. It's that simple.

[*Retrieving the chair, the COMMISSAR heads for the COUNTESS. She relinquishes NIKOLAI to VASNA and continues alone to stage center where she is tackled by the COMMISSAR in a knee-dropping dive.*]

THE COMMISSAR [*grabbing her ankles in prayerful anguish*]:
Make me a salesman! Make me a salesman!

COUNTESS IVANOVITCH [*jolted*]:
You're hurting my leg!

THE COMMISAR:
Send me to Kharkov—to Omsk—east of the Urals, I don't care!

[*During the commotion, a chalk-faced figure enters from the chapel. He is conspicuously outfitted in a loud sporty jacket and ascot. More conspicuous is his lack of trousers, his bare legs revealing his stock-in-trade garters at mid-calf. He heads for the street carrying an over-night bag with "AIR FRANCE" emblazoned on its side.*]

GYPSY JOE [*still dancing with the UNDERTAKER; gaping at the figure*]:
Don't look now, but your formaldehyde is showing.

THE COMMISSAR:
Make me free like a salesman!

COUNTESS IVANOVITCH [*with a conceding gesture*]:
I'll *send* you to Kharkov. But first, let go of my leg!

THE SPIRIT OF NODNIK [*to the COMMISSAR, flashing the AIR FRANCE logo*]:
Can I drop you?

THE COMMISSAR:
Are you heading west?

THE SPIRIT OF NODNIK [*highlighting the logo with his hand*]:
What does it look like?

THE COMMISSAR [*to UNDERTAKER*]:
How much time have we got?

UNDERTAKER [*glancing at the figure*]:
It's not of the essence.

THE COMMISSAR [*to the SPIRIT OF NODNIK*]:
Could you wait a few minutes. I got a stiff in the parlor.

[*The SPIRIT OF NODNIK leaves, closing the door behind him.*]

COUNTESS IVANOVITCH [*her back to the door*]:
What was that?

THE COMMISSAR:
Nothing, Countess Ivanovitch. Just a man without any pants. [*Taking the COUNTESS by the hand, they resume dancing.*]

COUNTESS IVANOVITCH:
Now this is my plan: Are you listening?

THE COMMISSAR [*on double-take*]:
Without any pants? I don't get it.

COUNTESS IVANOVITCH:
You will leave on the six-forty train from Noginsk. It will get you to Kharkov on Tuesday. I will arrange for a man who you will know by a shibboleth. Now there is every day in this racket a new shibboleth. So

164

whatever you do, don't be a slob in your speech. And remember—the one, most important, paramount thing: The customer is always right... The customer is always right...

[*The dance tempo increases as the music swells. The scene gradually dims to black.*]

The Meaning of Life

as delivered by a pitchman

for

The Polygrip & Spare Body Parts Society

The Meaning of Life

An aging, tassel-haired pitchman of dubious character and stamina works from behind a lectern. Beside the lectern is a small table holding a variety of props used in his demonstration.

Dear Friends and fellow members of the Polygrip and Spare Body Parts Society. It is with a *t-a-l-l* glass of pride that I stand before you—croissoned, I might add, by a touch of acidity. No, that isn't right. What rhymes with acidity? Humidity? Humility. Yes, Humility. With the crutch of humility that I stand before you...that I stand at all, if you stop to think about it. It's a miracle, actually—a ble-ble-blessed miracle. [*examining a scrap of paper*] In conclusion—no, that comes at the end. [*putting the paper back down*] I speak, that's it. I speak—not from the heart [*bringing his hand to his chest*] for obvious medical reasons—but from the lips. Yes, the lips...[*wetting his finger, putting it to his lips*] my lips...which makes sense.

[*attempting to unscramble his notes*] My topic today—if I can sort out the parts—the pieces—is one that should concern us all. I know it concerns me because I haven't the foggiest—oh, yes, I remember now—it had something to do with the meaning of life and what it means to those people who find it meaningful...which for reasons beyond my capacity to fathom—wound up in a spitball [*shaking his head in disbelief; half-mumbling*] ...wound up in a spitball.

[*stepping out in front of the lectern*] I had planned initially to talk about the organic infrastructure of the Akkadian oligarchy and its collapse in the year 2153 B.C. following an attempt to pollinate a rare strain of the hibiscus with the tsetse fly...and what it means to the tsetse fly. The word *tsetse*, as you undoubtedly know, comes from the word 'tsetse'— [*with exaggerated emphasis*] ZEET-SEE—which is annotative Italian for the Watusi mating call—done on a full stomach—and was known, even in pre-Latin times, as nodoso fumboso, mazarata, pizzicato, tutti-frutti, bungwat, tippy-poo—skut-but—corporealis nevi. But as you might have guessed, nobody could pronounce it—and that's what happened to the Akkadian oligarchy.

[*resuming his place behind the lectern, with book in hand*] I have here in my hand—yes, it is my hand—a copy, a true copy of the gospel according to Elizabeth Ashley Poindexter the 3rd who is thought to be the first Caucasian to cross the Gobi desert wearing only a pair of two-ply orthopedic arch supports. In the final chapter she reveals for the first time—and in her own inimitable words—she reveals the secret of— [*spitting something into his outstretched fingers*] caraway seeds— [*then forgetting his frame of reference*] which up to now has been closely guarded.

One of the great ironies of the gospel according to Elizabeth Ashley Poindexter the 3rd is that it was not *meant* to be a gospel. No-oo. It was, in fact, intended as a manual on Japanese garden tools. But it came to pass—as it often does—that in the year of the Kamikaze Goat [*looking heavenward*] a glob of Miracle Whip—some say bird droppings—infiltrated a batch of printer's ink and transformed a mundane piece of rot into what is now this priceless tome of ageless wisdom—which sells for $9.95 plus…[*with a perfunctory glance at his notes*] $15.00 to cover postage and handling…and [*picking up a small glass tube*] comes with this authentic vial of sanctified salt from the Dead Sea—which, when held in an upside-down position, actually defies gravity…[*demonstrating with negative results*] Well, most of the time it does…It also serves as a handy container for storing moth balls, old gall bladder stones—removed, of course—recycled bunion pads, things like that—a real bargain at $9.95 plus postage and handling.

169

[*reading from a scrap of paper*] Question: We have here a question. How many whiffs—I'll repeat that—how many whiffs of Ida Hogg's Prune Juice can you fit into a jar of loose catnip? *Loose* catnip? Hmmm, that *is* a conundrum. Well, I would think that would depend on the size of the jar. [*reading from another scrap of paper*] Lord, have mercy! What have we here? A joke. Not one, but three. Three unbelievably tasteless jokes—never used by Joan Rivers. Actually, they're from the private collection of the Archbishop of Cloistersham who, in a fit of ecumenical compassion—brought on by mounting gambling debts—sold them to a destitute Hollywood gag writer for the then unheard-of sum of six pounds, four shillings, which included, I understand, a pair of cuff links that once belonged to John Gilbert—the highest amount ever paid, not withstanding the cuff links, for a joke on designer panty hose—also part of the private collection of the Archbishop of Cloistersham.

The meaning of life—ah, yes—and what it means to those who find it meaningful. I suppose that's something you've all wondered about—haven't you? Between trips to the podiatrist—or in moments of grief—or in moments of grief and *then* trips to the podiatrist. It's times like these that make us pause and look into ourselves—into those dark recesses of what it is that's recessed—which, I grant, is a matter of some debate. Not everyone agrees, for example, that there *is* a soul, or that it can be replaced—or do they know that such a bank exists in the spare parts division of our computerized holistic clinic—each and every one, I might add, individually tailored to the exact specifications of one's karma. It's the kind of software I suspect you've all been looking for but couldn't find. Well, the good news my friends, my fellow members of the Polygrip and Spare Body Parts Society, the good news is that it's here now, beautifully illustrated in this [*holding up a brochure*] state-of-the-art platitude—uh, catalogue—which for your convenience has the unique feature of being indexed spectroscopically [*opening the brochure to reveal an enlarged light spectrum*] according to the natural tint of one's aura—the blue end of

170

the spectrum, [*fingering the blue band*] of course, denoting the super achievers, those who managed to claw their way to the top—the rest of us falling more or less into the red, you see here, the red—some—into the black [*fingering the black*] —less fortunate, of course. It all depends on where you're coming from, you see. You *do* see that? Not to seem pushy or anything, but I would recommend that you order your replacement now while the supply lasts, particularly those of you in the ultraviolet range which seems to be the trend this year—upward mobility and all that. For those of you in the hot zone—that's the white part [*illustrating*] where the color runs out, kind of parched looking— we've included at no additional cost an automatic icemaker, fully warranted for the life of the product—or fifty thousand ice cubes, whichever comes first.

[*stepping out from behind the lectern*] And now the cost: That's something you've wondered about, I'm sure. Some people would say if you have to ask the price, you can't afford it. Well, in this case, they're right. There are some things in this world that are beyond value and I would think your soul would be one of them. It's not something you can simply put a tag on llke a box of jelly tarts or a bag of Taupper's Mini Mints, you see...or is it Nettie Norton's Mini Mints? The pink ones in the blue wrapper?...It's not blue anymore? They changed the wrapper, you don't say. [*shaking his head, muttering to himself*] Changed the wrapper...Then, too, some people wouldn't want you to know they even needed one—a soul, that is—at any price. It's a matter of personal pride, like having your face lifted—or your rump reduced— or your jowls upgraded. Some people do that, you know. They tie rubber bands around their ears to hold up their jowls to keep them from falling—and they don't want you to know—until it snaps. Then it's too late. Well, it's like that with the soul. You wouldn't want people to know that it snapped, much less what you paid for it.

171

[*returning to the lectern, removing a pen from his pocket and placing it alongside a blank sheet of paper*] Now, if you'll be kind enough to leave your name and phone number, I'll get back to you as soon as I get to a phone booth. We—ah—don't have an office right now, I'm sorry to say. It—ah—blew up…yes…It was on a Tuesday, I think. Was it a Tuesday? Yes, it was a Tuesday. They said we were free-basing nitroglycerin but that wasn't it at all. No, it was a bad batch of souls that did it. Blew the oven door right off. Hit an Episcopalian and an Airedale. Pedigree, too. A real shame. What made it worse, they arrested us. Said we were operating without a license, can you beat that? Put me in the slammer, they did—in the jail house—in a cold, cold cell with a hardened criminal…Of course, he was frozen to death…I told the man at the desk, I said, you know, we—we—we could use some heat in this here place. I don't mind the icicles but I can't get my teeth out of the glass. Well, it took thirty days and a Mac-6 blowtorch to thaw me out. It just doesn't pay to be born some days, it really doesn't. If it wasn't for those spare body parts and the reclamation of souls and the gospel according to what's-her-name—I don't know as I'd care to go on living. The real meaning of life, I guess, is that there isn't any meaning. There was this Arab fellow—Omar Khayyam, I think—who sent his soul through the invisible, he did—and when it returned—he couldn't even see it. That tells you something.

Well, if I can't reach you by phone, maybe I'll see you in the next life…That's a juice bar around the corner. I always get my goat's milk there and my rutabaga tips dipped in chocolate. You should try it sometime. It's good for the waistline. It's called the Automatic Reflux Diet. It's ejected before it reaches the stomach…Well, it's been nice talking to you, it really has. You've been a true and dedicated bunch and the Lord love you for your souls. But should you ever need a new one—or just a simple retooling job—you know where to reach me. In the meantime, you keep those body parts moving, you hear? You do that now [*gathering up his props*] 'cause that's what it's all about. Yessir, that's what it's all about. [*He exits with a doddering wave.*]

172

I Thought I was in Love

with Nietzsche

as told and sung
by
Pamela Crankshaft

Music was composed originally for the lyric portion and is available from the publisher on request. As an option, the set can be done without piano accompaniment, with the performer improvising the melody.

I Thought I was in Love with Nietzsche

PAMELA, a mod type with long, straight hair, large owl-like glasses and a deadpan demeanor, is languishing on a high stool near a piano, singing:

> A year ago it came to me
> That I was quite superior,
> And so it followed naturally
> That other people were inferior.

[She removes her glasses, revealing garish eye makeup, then proceeds to clean her glasses with a tissue.]

I bet you think I'm rather strange, don't you—telling you what a superior creature I am. I mean you resent it, even if it is true. And it is, you know. I don't know why I should go around pretending to be ordinary when it's so obvious I'm not.

[Putting her glasses back on, she blows her nose with the tissue and resumes singing:]

> Now I don't mean to offend you
> But the facts of life are these:
> That some are born to pedigree
> And some to pick the fleas.

I was always one of those hush hush things you don't mention in polite company. She's superior—oh, my god!—like I had morning mouth or something. I always say 'if we don't have it ourselves we should at least recognize it in others.' Goethe had the right idea. He used to say, "What can you do about superior but admire it." He was referring to genius, of course. I don't mean anything so banal as an IQ of 200, but the genius of insight that gave us relativity or [*Insert name of a well known mediocrity.*] —that incandescent something that illuminates the very depths of the human soul.

My own case was quite similar. I was always the peculiar one, probing the deep and illicit waters. "Pamela," I would say, "what are you living for? Why were you born? What is the meaning of it all?" I was desperate for an answer but pleased also that I was asking such intelligent questions. People wondered about me. "That Pamela, she's a peculiar one. She probes the deep and illicit waters." Well, why shouldn't I? I was lonely. I was always lonely—even as a child. I had no parents, you see. They died...[*Wiping her nose, sniffling.*] Well, I killed them actually...[*Then dropping the tissue to the floor.*] I didn't mean to pour gasoline on them, but it was fun to watch...[*Singing:*]

> The following year when I was six
> And entered grammar school...

It was at the tender age of six that I began to notice I was different from other little girls and boys. They were adjusted, well-meaning, good natured. I was obnoxious. They wanted me to play hopscotch and pussy cat. But what did I care about hopscotch and pussy cat. I was too busy reading Nietzsche. *Free-der-rik* Nietzsche. I wanted to be absolutely certain I was despising the right things, to know there was at least one other soul who shared my disdain for the human race. It was wonderful. A whole new vista of loathing was opened to me. At last I could hate with a clean feeling. [*Singing:*]

> When I discovered Nietzsche
> My head was out of reach-ee,
> I was tanked on Super Permalube.

I THOUGHT I WAS IN LOVE WITH NIETZSCHE

I didn't need a booster,
I had Zarathuster,
Gravity was just a platitude.

I found myself a new dimension,
Unaffected by convention
Or the laws enslaving ordinary minds.
I strained at self-surpassing
Till I attained the everlasting
And sailed right out of space and time.

Oh, it was heaven-lee divine!

I think I knew happiness for the first time. I don't mean just happiness.
I mean *happiness.* God, I was happy. Wherever I went people would
say, "There goes Pamela Crankshaft. Isn't she happy?" They were
extremely envious of my relationship with Free-der-rik. They said I
was eating Mexican mushrooms and Peyote cactus, that I was
pharmacologically unsound. But what did I care. I was too exalted to
bother. I went on being exalted for six wonderful years, followed by
five years of unutterable bliss and three years of indescribable
ecstasy...I was exhausted...I wanted to kill myself but I was laughing
so much I kept missing my veins. Every day, the same delirious,
unrelenting happiness. I began to wonder if total fulfillment was
all I had a right to expect. Then one day as I sat there, picking the
charcoal off my nerve endings—delirious as usual—I felt a strange new
presence, a magical sound I never heard before. Suddenly, I didn't love
Nietzsche anymore. I loved somebody else. Somebody new. [*Singing:*]

I thought I was in love with Nietzsche
Until I met Lawrence Welk,
Now it's a rivederci, Free-der-rik Nare-chee,
Hello, Larry Welk!

When he smiles at me I feel so leechy,
I could jump right up and screechee—

[*She leaps from the stool with a screech, then breaks into a freestyle
dance involving wild body contortions.*]

Who would have thought that bourgeois love
Could be so grand.

Oh, he's the darling of my aviary,
Good old champagne Larry,
I'm in love, I'm in love with—
A wonderful man!

Now life is peachy,
To hell with Nietzsche,
Larry is my man!

[*Blackout.*]

Nibblets

or

Characters I once knew

Nibblets

I don't know whether I should even tell you this; you're apt to think I've tainted my jellybeans—but I'll tell you anyway. It's what I do with my spare time—when I'm sober—which is mostly on Tuesdays and Thursdays. What *do* I do with my spare time? Well, I don't reshingle my tool shed, that's for sure—because I don't have one. And I don't ring church bells anymore or make Fatty Arbuckle window stoppers, if you know what that is—and if you don't, it won't change your life. What I do is, I write poetry—nothing elaborate, just little four-liners I call nibblets. I call them that because you can't really swallow them whole; they have to be nibbled at. And I dedicate these poems, these nibblets, to people I once knew. I say that because if they still knew me, they'd kill me. Each week I try to pick a new subject, something light and frivolous, not too frilly—maybe a bit on the fluffy side, but not frilly. This week I thought I'd go with *Death and Suicide*—that's always been a winner with poets, particularly the young ones who seem to enjoy expounding on matters they don't feel especially threatened by.

My first one is about a fellow named Merton. Merton was into philosophy—he liked philosophy. He was also a bit of a snoot. By that I mean, he didn't just like any philosopher. He was careful to select only those that were in fashion. George Santayana, he thought was kind of groovy. He was popular in the early eighties—eighty-one, eighty-two—until November of eighty-four when he fell out of favor. Philosophers are like that, you see. They're like vintage wine. They're good some years, but not others. He also liked Milton. Every spring he would go around with a copy of *Paradise Lost* and then in the fall he would switch to *Paradise Regained.* Why he gummed up the seasons, metaphorically at least, I'll never know. But that was Merton. He was kind of perverse that way. He didn't believe much in tradition. In fact, he didn't believe much in anything. He was what you call an up-in-the-air kind of person. For him everything was in a state of limbo, nothing really congealed. In fact, his whole world was like an undercooked pudding. You couldn't really sink your teeth into it; you had to slurp it—and then hope you didn't dribble. I had a name for it. I called it agnostic cuisine. He wasn't even sure what he was sure about—except maybe Heisenberg's Principle of Uncertainty and I'm not sure he was too certain about that. It was a dreary, unsettled world he was living in, where nothing happened, or could happen, or would you know about it even if it did. I think he once referred to it as a nuisance—like it was interrupting his eternal sleep. I often wondered why he didn't just pull the plug and call it a day. Anyway, in my poem I sort of suggested that he did, and that he went to his maker, as improbable at that may sound. And how fitting it would be, these words, if tacked on his tombstone— like an epitaph. And this is what I wrote—to the tragic and unfinished Merton...

> Alas, aloof, in death he hangs,
> Betwixt the stars and grass, poor Merton;
> For earth he found was much too shallow,
> And heaven too uncertain.

I had another friend who I call my Asian friend. He was a real dyed-in-the-wool Hindu—from India—which is where they come from, you know, Hindus—at least most of them do. Well, he wasn't just a Hindu. He was a Brahman—which if you know anything about Hindus is the top of the line. And he believed in reincarnation, as Hindus do—or most of them anyway. But with him it wasn't just a belief, it was a passion—which is kind of unusual because most Hindus don't believe that much in passion. Well, he came to this country, my friend did, to study engineering, which is what they do, the Hindus, or Brahmans, they're all engineers, most of them. Well, he wasn't here very long and, lo and behold, he became a Baptist. Not just a Baptist, but a dyed-in-the-wool, born-again Baptist, which for a Baptist, I guess, is the top of the line. So when I saw him again, I asked him—his name, I think, was Clarence—which I thought was kind of odd for a Hindu, but that was his name—I asked him about reincarnation, did he still believe in it. And he said "no"—that as a Baptist he would have to go straight to heaven—no stopovers for refueling—things like that, you see. Well, he didn't go to heaven, at least directly. He went back to India and that's the last I ever heard of him. But I often wonder about my friend Clarence, if he ever reconverted, or if he didn't, how he could reconcile his being born-again and not believe in reincarnation. And so I wrote this little poem which I dedicated to my friend, my Asian friend from Asia...

> There once was an Asian of a certain persuasion,
> Who chopped his way through to the final equation;
> And when he was buried and returned as a biscuit,
> Was ever so sure that he never existed.

The next one doesn't really involve suicide although it could after you hear it. When I was young, as most people are sometime in their life, and we finished our schooling, or left the cherished confines of the parental nest, or were evicted as the case may be—into the river of life, we didn't leapfrog as they do today into fancy four-room flats or townhouses in the suburbs or chateaux in the Pyrenees, or whatever—no, we went through what was called the rooming house stage. You don't see too many of them around anymore. They've sort of disappeared from the landscape. A shame, too, because living in one was like taking a postgraduate course in life; you learned things you never learned in school.

But to get on with my story. It's a fact known to poets and philosophers alike, and to men of knowledge generally, that in the entire history of mankind there has never been a rooming house that wasn't owned and operated by a landlady. Civilizations come and go, they convulse and die or go into shock, and there, groping her way through the rubble, is the landlady, collecting her rent. She's been immortalized by every writer that's ever lived—or maybe I should say 'demortalized.' She's had a singularly bad press. Why that should be, I don't know. There's been some good ones. I guess it goes back to Dostoyevski and his *Crime and Punishment*. It was certainly true of most young writers of my generation. They had two things in this world they despised. One was the devil, the other was their landlady—due mainly I suspect to cultural differences and the fact that they couldn't pay their rent.

Well, anyway, there was this one that I knew—which in all fairness to the historic tradition was in the mainstream of witchhood. She owned not one, but a whole string of rooming houses and her name was Mrs. Lawson. I called her Gypsy Lawson because she lived in a cave. Well, not a cave, exactly. It was a small room in back of one of her buildings. It was dark like a cave, though; more like a pit, really. I called it the black hole because if you ever got sucked into it, you'd never come out. She had this thing about electricity, you see. She didn't believe in it—I guess because it cost money. Well, it was the custom in those days that you paid your rent like once a week, on a Tuesday or so, and so you would go to her door, her chamber door, and do a tap, tap, tap like the raven, and the door would open and out of this pit, this black hole, would come this claw that would grab onto the rent money and then disappear into the void. How she could tell a five from a ten, I'll never know. It's one of those rare talents that only landladies possess.

She had another peculiar habit. She would go around at night with a flashlight and check on her tenants to see who was using up her electricity, or exceeding the one kilowatt hour she allotted each month—or worse—if they had the temerity to replace one of her 25-

watt bulbs with a 30, then she would increase their rent like a dollar a week or so. I was a struggling writer then or at least fancied myself as such (when I wasn't working as a bricklayer's assistant) and was prone to burn the midnight oil, so, needless to say, I became one of her prime targets for these rent increases. She kept increasing my rent a dollar a week until finally I had to move to the Waldorf Astoria—or was it the Waldorfs *in* Astoria? Anyway, before I did, I tacked this little poem on her door. I don't know if she ever saw it or if she even knew who wrote it. I rather doubt it because I don't think she could read. Anyway, I thought I would rededicate this poem to her, wherever she is. If she's still living, she'd be 120 next month...

> The night was owned by Gypsy Lawson,
> The stars she owned as well,
> Until one night she shut them off to save the juice,
> And blasted heaven into hell.

So much for Mrs. Lawson.

This is the final one and then I'll call it a day. It doesn't involve anyone I know so I won't bore you with a lot of detail. I call it *Ode to a Manic-depressive*. I was going to call it *Ode to a Suicidal Manic-depressive* but I thought that might sound a bit too fluffy...

> Sad is the tale, and sadder the pain,
> Of a manic-depressive on Suicide Lane;
> As hard as she tried, she never quite died,
> She was laughing so much, she kept missing her vein.

Poor Li'l Crocodile

To Edna - with fond remembrance

Poor Li'l Crocodile

*The scene opens on a dimly-lit tavern with a honky-tonk piano as
background. The light increases slowly, focusing on an aging barfly,
a throwback to the flapper era with cloche hat and overly accented
bee-stung lips, clutching a gin bottle in one hand, a glass in the other.
She has the heroic quality of someone oblivious to a world that kept
on spinning long after she got off—or perhaps was thrown off. There
is an underlying bitterness in her tone but there are moments when
she is almost queenly sublime, manifesting a certain brazen magnifi-
cence that comes from the small, but hard-fought, victories the poor
sometimes obtain in their unending battle with adversity.*

*It is the wee hours of the morning and she is by now thoroughly
lubricated. A purse and the remnants of a once-proud fly swatter
languish nearby.*

[*Emptying the bottle into the glass.*] You don't have to say it. I know
what you're thinking. She's no damn good. Well, you're right for once.
I'm just an old booze hound that never got started on the right foot. I
don't tell this to everybody 'cause I think everybody should find out
for themselves. That's what I believe. If you're gonna survive, you
gotta face the facts and the fact is, I'm just one hell of a mess.

[*She hits the table with the fly swatter.*]

The dirty crocodiles. Can't even drink in peace without those slimy
things creepin' up on you. Try that again you lousy lizard and I'll ram
this right down your lateral chasmatic.

186

POOR LI'L CROCODILE

[Laying the swatter aside, she drinks up.]

Interruptions, interruptions. What is life anyway—but a farce. From the first burp to the last—just a lot of petroleum, that's all that it is.

[She half-consciously tips the empty bottle into the glass.]

Personally, I don't care if it's good or bad, if it's right or wrong or left or right. All this to-do they're making about what to do and what not to do and when is the best time not to do it—I don't go for that stuff. Nosiree. I'll just go along breathin' the air—what there is of it—and when there isn't any air, I'll quit breathin' and I won't be mad at nobody—not even the evilest man in the whole world.

[She takes a swig, then wipes her mouth with the swatter.]

I don't say I'm above all this commotion 'cause if I did I'd be a damn liar. By that I don't mean I'm not a damn liar. I'm the biggest liar that every lived but I don't mean to be a liar. I believe in truth, that's what I believe. I think there should be more of it. I believe life should be a bed of roses and all the roses should be equal. That's my philosophy, Roses for everybody!

[She takes another drink; with increasing giddiness.]

Don't give a damn. Don't care. Just go along—smile at the world and the world will smile at you. And god bless every man, woman and child in the star-spangled spates and the histhmus of Panama.

[Laughing fiendishly, she tips the bottle to the glass once again. A few drops trickle out. Her laughter stops instantly.]

Well, I'll be a dirty doodle.

187

[*She turns the bottle around so the label faces away.*]

It's colorless!

[*Looking back towards an imaginary bar:*]

Bartender!

[*A brief pause.*]

Bartender!

[*She stomps the table with the bottle. Another pause. She takes the swatter in hand and peers over the table's edge.*]

You're not the bartender. You're a cheap, lousy crocodile and you'll always be one if you live to be seven thousand, eight hundred and—

[*Suddenly looking up, as if to the bartender:*]

Oh, there you are, you old plug wit. I've been calling you since yesterday morning. Where in the name of heaven have you been? You don't say. Well, now that you're here you can remove this bottle before I regurgitate.

[*Transferring the bottle to a remote section of the table:*]

Whaddaya mean, what's wrong? Look at it, you chromy-eyed bat.

[*Revolving the bottle with disdain so the label faces in:*]

It's crawling with convalescence. When I want an eyewash I'll go to an apothecary. If there's a sick microbe in the house, they label it. And don't tell me to pipe down or I'll swat you. I don't care if it is closing

188

time which it isn't 'cause it isn't even daylight yet and you can juggle
your skillet on that one, by truly, or you can go to hell on a gondola
which is a far, far better thing than you'll ever do—in any case.

[*Looking back, shouting:*]

You dirty hustler!

[*Aside, with dead earnestness:*]

That's all they are is a bunch of hustlers. They hustle you in and they
hustle you out till you're so damn hustled you don't know a pitch pipe
from a Presbyterian and that is the truth.

[*The piano returns with a rendering of "Blow the Man Down." She
removes a mirror from her purse and starts primping as she sings:*]

"As I was walking down Paradise Street,
   Way! Hey! Blow the man down..."

Don't give a damn. Don't care. Just go along, livin' it up till I die. Like
I say, I'm just an old booze hound that never quite found the mark. It
isn't that I didn't try 'cause god only knows I did the best I could. I
was decent and respectable and—and everything that a good girl
should be. But you know what I found out?

[*Returning the mirror to her purse; to the house, confidentially:*]

It doesn't pay. It never has and it never will. It's a rotten, no-good
civilization—

[*Closing her purse, then a slight pause as her solemn demeanor gives
way to a wry smile:*]

But I love it! I really do. I think it's just wonderful and I'm so glad, just thrilled to pieces that I can stand up in a public place and say what a mess I think it's made of me. That's something. When you can stand up in a public place and tell the world what a god-forsaken mess you are.

[*She is on her feet, slapping her thigh.*]

Isn't it wonderful? Well, isn't it?

[*She raps the table with the swatter.*]

Aw, go to hell, you dirty crocodile!

[*A pause while she surveys the table.*]

Crocodile? Oh, crocodile.

[*She looks away; with surprised hurt:*]

Somebody stole my crocodile.

[*Peering under the table and the nearby floor:*]

Here, Crocodile. Here I am.

[*Slowly her eyes revert to the swatter still in her hand. Then a look of mournfulness:*]

Poor li'l crocodile. What a terrible mess you are.

[*She presses the swatter to her heart. The scene dims slowly to black.*]

STREET UNNAMED

CHARACTERS

CHARLOTTE

MAX

STREET VENDOR

QUEEN

CHRIS

SKIP

LARRY

POP

MADGE

SCENE: *A tavern on an 'unnamed' street*

STREET UNNAMED

The interior of a shabby gin mill. At far right is a door to the street (now open) and, up center, a wall sign reading GREEN LANTERN. At the far end of the room is a dilapidated bar with wooden stools and scattered throughout are several tables and chairs just as dilapidated.

It is early evening. A woman is at the bar talking to MAX, the bartender. Two young men and an older man with a crutch are seated at separate tables. The sound of an off-stage nickelodeon carries under the opening lines.

CHARLOTTE:
So he tells her, Max, "I don't care if you walk the streets naked!" So yesterday morning, mind you, she comes walking down the street with not even a pair of shoes on. They can't take her nowhere, Mark and Eddie, so they call the station. Well, in the meantime the crowd is getting bigger and bigger. So what does Mark and Eddie do but wrap her up in the Racing Form. [*Climactically.*] Well, it wasn't big enough to go around…It was the funniest thing you ever saw, Max. [*She emits a hearty laugh.*]

MAX:
They lock her up?

CHARLOTTE:
Naw. They sent her up for another examination. But don't you worry. She'll be back tomorrow. They ain't got room enough in those wards.

[*A man appears in the doorway with a handful of pamphlets.*]

193

STREET VENDOR:
Jesus saves. Jesus saves. Jesus saves.

MAX:
Nix, bub. Get yourself another beat.

[*A short, overdressed lady wearing a tiara and carrying a magazine appears at the doorway but is blocked from entering.*]

QUEEN:
Pardon me, Jack.

STREET VENDOR:
Would you like to know Jesus?

QUEEN:
Will he buy me a drink?

MAX [*to the VENDOR*]:
I said 'scram.'

[*The VENDOR leaves as QUEEN enters.*]

STREET VENDOR [*off*]:
Believe in Jesus for he is our savior.

QUEEN:
Ain't a bad lookin' guy, Max. Who is he?

MAX:
Who knows. One of Sister Carrie's converts maybe.

QUEEN [*to one of the young men as she passes*]:
Hello, kid.

CHRIS:
Hello, yourself. How ya doin'?

QUEEN [*in her adopted 'Mae West' persona*]:
I'm doin' okay. Who's the friend?

CHRIS [*to SKIP*]:
Skip, I want you to meet Fannie, queen of the honkytonks.

[*SKIP extends his hand in greeting.*]

QUEEN [*responding in kind after checking her nails*]:
You'll hafta excuse. I ain't had time to have 'em manicured.

CHRIS:
She used to own a cabaret up the street, didn't you, Queen.

QUEEN:
Up the street, down the street, who cares. I owned the whole goddamn
street, didn't I, Max.

MAX:
You sure did.

QUEEN:
And fix me a beer while you're at it.

MAX [*obliging*]:
Sure thing, Fannie.

QUEEN [*to CHRIS, confidentially*]:
Save your friend. I might wanna use him some time—in real estate.
[*She slinks seductively to a far table and sits.*]

195

SKIP:
What a crock. Is she for real?

CHRIS:
She was once. Had money, lots of it. Then something happened, I don't know what. But it hit her kinda hard 'cause now she goes around thinking she's queen of the street. Someone dug up that old tiara to humor her and she's been wearing it ever since.

SKIP:
You know something, Chris—

CHRIS:
Yeah, what?

SKIP:
The street. It should have a better name.

CHRIS:
The name's alright.

SKIP:
No, on the level. It ain't dynamic enough.

CHRIS:
Dynamic?

SKIP:
Yeah, that's it—dynamic—something with fire in it to bring out its character. That's what it needs.

CHRIS:
You want fire? How about Furnace Avenue. That's a good name.

SKIP:
Naw, that's not what I mean.

CHRIS:
Better drink your beer, chum. It's getting late.

[*A man enters from the street and goes straight to the bar. He has the dress and appearance of a street thug.*]

LARRY:
You ain't seen Madge around, have you, Max?

MAX:
Not tonight, Larry.

LARRY:
If she comes in, tell her I'm lookin' for her.

MAX:
Sure thing.

LARRY:
And tell her I ain't kiddin' this time. I mean it good. [*He exits.*]

CHRIS:
Who's Madge?

MAX:
Some dame used to work here.

CHRIS:
And who, may I inquire, is the gentleman?

MAX:
Can't you tell? That's her old man. At least he claims he is.

CHRIS:
Poor Madge.

MAX [*wiping the bar*]:
Yeah, she got married and she quit. That is, she quit workin'. You probably seen her around but never noticed. Sits over there [*Pointing to an empty table.*] with another guy and a friend.

CHRIS:
What's she doin' here if she's got a husband?

MAX:
Now, ain't that one for the books. What's anyone doin' here?

[*POP, the old-timer, gets up from a center table and walks over to the young men. He has a slight limp. He is also slightly drunk.*]

POP:
That's a good queshon, gentlemen. That's a very good queshon. Now take me for instance.

CHRIS:
Sit down, old-timer.

POP [*obliging*]:
Whad am I doing here? You know, that's a very good queshon. What am I doing here?

CHRIS:
You're here because you ain't got no place else to go, right, Pop?

198

POP:
I'm a reasonably cultured man. I got a whole lotta degrees from some university. Maybe you heard of it—but I forgot. You didn't know that, did you, boys? Yezsir. And I got an ezhacational background too!

CHRIS [*to SKIP*]:
Sit tight, chum. This is a long story.

POP:
Max knows I went to a university because I told him. Didn't I tell you, Max? Didn't I tell you I went to a university?

MAX:
You sure did.

POP:
There, you see? Whaddaya say to that?

CHRIS:
So whatcha doin' here. Why aren't you in politics?

POP:
Because I'm a respectable man, that's why—an' I don't like to be insulted. [*Rising, he rests his hands on the table for support.*]

CHRIS:
Nobody's insulting you.

POP:
Then don't ever ask whad I'm doin' around here because I got jus' as much right az anybody. Yezsir. This place is as mush mine as it is yourz or Max's or the Duke of Paducah hizself. God bless the dirty bastard! [*Hitting the table clumsily with his fist, he is helped back to his seat.*]

199

[*A woman in obvious distress enters from the street carrying a purse. She is in her forties, sans makeup, but dressed for a better place. Her hair falls back uncombed, accenting her unsettled state.*]

MADGE [*nervously*]:
Hello, Max.

MAX:
Hey, Madge, Larry was just here lookin' for you.

MADGE:
I know.

MAX:
He didn't sound too good. What's up?

MADGE:
Give me a shot.

MAX:
Maybe you better lay off.

MADGE [*with an intensity*]:
Give me a shot.

MAX:
Sure. Sure.

MADGE:
Bugs hasn't been around, has he?

MAX:
No, Madge.

MADGE:
What's the matter with him anyway? What about Grace?

MAX:
She ain't been around either.

MADGE [*dramatically*]:
Max, I'm leaving.

MAX:
Yeah?

MADGE:
I know, I said that before. I mean it this time.

MAX [*filling a shot glass; offering it to MADGE*]:
Is that why he's after you?

MADGE [*drinking up*]:
He's out to kill me this time. Yeah, that's what he said. He's out to kill me. [*Laughing sardonically.*] Isn't that ridiculous? Well, he's a ridiculous guy.

POP:
Hello, Madge.

MADGE [*turns, facing POP*]:
Well, hello, old-timer.

POP:
Come over here and sit, Madge. I got two very nice gentlemen I would like you to meet.

MADGE:
Not now, Pop.

201

POP:
Whazzamadder, Madge? Don't you like me anymore?

MADGE:
No, I'm in a hurry. [*To MAX.*] You're sure you ain't seen either one of them?

MAX:
I told you, 'no.'

MADGE:
Christ, why can't they come. [*She empties the shot glass.*] You know I'm leaving, Max.

MAX:
Sure.

MADGE:
I'm getting outta here. I bet I sound funny, don't I? I bet nobody ever thought I was gonna leave this place.

MAX:
You don't belong here, Madge.

MADGE:
Oh, you can be funny, too. [*Laughing.*] I don't belong here, he sez. That's a good one! I got my stamp all over this street. Everybody knows me. Everybody on the street, they know me, and I don't belong here? Then where the hell do I belong? Tell me that!

MAX:
Madge, keep it down. We got customers.

MADGE:
Ain't I a customer? No, I guess maybe I'm not. Maybe I'm nothing! The Street of Forgotten People, isn't that what they call it? Well, I'm one of those people the world forgot. But I'm not gonna stay forgot because I'm leaving, see. I'm gonna leave you, Max, and I'm gonna leave Pop over there, and I'm gonna leave this whole damn rotten world! [*She shoves the empty glass towards MAX.*] You gotta make room for the new ones, isn't that right, Pop?

POP [*gently*]:
That's right, Madge—room for the new ones.

MADGE:
That's why I came here—just to say goodbye. I couldn't leave without saying goodbye, could I? I mean they wouldn't think that was right, would they?

MAX:
Madge, take a tip from me. Larry's comin' back. I don't want you here when he comes.

MADGE:
I understand. I'll go—just as soon as they come. Give me another one.

MAX:
No more.

MADGE [*shoving a loose bill towards MAX*]:
I got money.

MAX [*shoving the money back*]:
No drinks.

MADGE:
I gotta have a drink! Please. Please, Max.

[*MAX walks away, ignoring her.*]

You wanna know something, Max? Larry ain't no good. You wanna know something else?

MAX:
No.

MADGE:
What's the matter, Max?

MAX:
You're tight.

MADGE:
No, I'm not.

MAX:
No, you're not tight. It's just my imagination.

MADGE:
You wanna know something else about Larry?

MAX:
Sure. Sure, I got all night.

MADGE:
He's got a gun and he's after me.

MAX [*unconcerned*]:
Yeah?

MADGE:
Because I saw him kill a man tonight.

[*MAX gives her a half-startled look while busying himself at the bar.*]

Sure. He killed a man. You'll be surprised when I tell you who it was. It was Charlie.

MAX:
Charlie? Charlie who?

MADGE:
You don't know Charlie? I thought everybody knew Charlie.

MAX:
Can't say I do, Madge?

MADGE [*picking her purse up from the bar*]:
That's why I'm leaving, Max. I can't stay here no more or he'll get me. He'll get me like he got all the rest.

MAX:
The rest?

MADGE:
Yes, all of us. You and me and everybody. He'll get everybody but he won't get me because I'm too smart. I'm getting out.

MAX:
Whaddaya mean, 'he'll get everybody'?

MADGE:
He just will, that's all.

MAX:
Who? Larry?

MADGE [*screaming*]:
I don't know who. He doesn't have a name!

MAX:
Listen to me, Madge. You're not making any sense.

MADGE:
Don't scream at me. [*Pathetically.*] Give me another, Max.

MAX:
I said 'no more.'

MADGE:
I gotta have a drink.

MAX [*a change of heart, he pours a refill*]:
Okay, okay, but this is it.

MADGE:
Thanks. Oh, thanks, Max. [*Drinking up.*] You're a swell guy, Max. [*She turns from the bar, walking away with the half-empty shot glass.*]

MAX:
Where you goin'?

MADGE:
I'm gonna wait for Bugs.

MAX:
I thought you were in a hurry.

MADGE:
I gotta say goodbye, don't I? What kinda person you think I am—don't say goodbye to my friends. If you see Larry, tell him I left. Would you do me that favor, Max?

MAX:
If he doesn't see you first.

MADGE:
And tell him I didn't tell nobody. Would you do that, Max?

MAX:
Sure.

MADGE:
Thanks. [*Setting her glass on the bar, she heads for the table occupied by CHRIS, SKIP and POP, stopping on the way to rummage through her purse.*] My cigarettes are all gone. Anyone here got a cigarette?

[*CHRIS offers her a cigarette. The nickelodeon returns but remains in in the background.*]

Thanks. You don't mind if I sit down, do you?

CHRIS:
Go right ahead.

MADGE:
I'm waiting for some friends.

CHRIS:
Oh?

MADGE [*a pause, while trying to light up*]:
Have you got any friends?

CHRIS:
Sure. Lots of 'em.

MADGE:
I got some friends. Two of them—two real good friends and I'm waiting for them.

CHRIS [*offering assistance to MADGE who has been unable to light her cigarette*]
Here, let me light that for you.

MADGE:
Because, you see, I lost a friend. Somebody I knew for a long, long time. They—they shot him—Larry did. Larry and everybody shot him. But now they're all afraid. They think I'm going to tell, but I'm not because, you see, Larry didn't know what he was doing. So I'm leaving and I came to say goodbye. [*Gazing into a small mirror she has removed from her purse.*] Gee, I don't look so nice, do I? [*Rummaging through her purse again.*] Where's my comb? I've gotta comb my hair. [*Finding a broken comb, she offers it to CHRIS.*] Would you comb my hair? Here, comb it a few times, would you, Jack. That's you name— Jack—isn't it?

CHRIS:
You better put the comb away, lady.

MADGE [*bringing the comb through her hair, crudely*]:
Oh, no. No, not the way I am. I couldn't go away like this. Would you put the lamp on so I can see.

CHRIS:
There's no lamp.

208

MADGE:
No, there's no light at all—only from the music box and that's a very dim light.

[*The lights dim as the sound from the nickelodeon draws nearer. MADGE shifts the mirror from one spot to another.*]

It must be the days are getting shorter. In a little while the old nickelodeon will be the strongest light in the city. Then we can all dig in for a long winter's nap and let the music lull us to sleep with its velvety lights. I like it when the music dances. You like the music when it dances?

CHRIS:
Sometimes.

MADGE:
I like music. I like it real well. And Charlie, he was nuts about music. Why, he could play a trumpet like you never heard it played. You remember, Charlie, don't you, Pop?

POP:
I'm afraid I don't, Madge.

MADGE:
You don't remember Charlie? I thought everyone knew Charlie.

POP:
No, who is he, Madge?

MADGE:
I can't believe that no one here remembers.

CHRIS:
Was he a close friend?

MADGE:
Yes, he was—a very close friend.

CHRIS:
How long have you known him?

MAX:
Hey, Madge, you better go.

MADGE [*putting the comb and mirror back in her purse*]:
I wonder where they could be. I have to say goodbye.

MAX:
Yeah, I know, Madge. How about if I tell them for you?

MADGE [*Getting up; overly grateful*]:
Would you do that?

MAX:
Sure, I'll be glad to.

MADGE:
Oh, you're swell, Max. Tell them how really sorry I am. And that I could've stayed except for Larry. [*She crosses to the door.*]

MAX:
Sure.

[*She exits to the street. Voices from a nearby tabernacle can be heard in the background singing "Glory to His Name." A slight pause, after which MADGE reenters and races for the bar.*]

MADGE [*panicky*]:
Max, quick, give me a drink.

210

MAX:
What's up?

MADGE:
Larry—

MAX:
Larry?

MADGE:
He's coming!

MAX:
Get in back. I'll tell 'im—

MADGE:
No, Max. He saw me.

MAX [*hurriedly grabbing a nearby liquor glass, filling it*]:
Jesus.

MADGE:
Quick, I gotta think.

MAX:
Here, Madge. Take this.

[*LARRY enters with a swagger*]:

LARRY [*ominously*]:
Hello, Madge.

MADGE [*turning, with glass in hand*]:
Stay away from me, Larry.

211

LARRY:
What's the matter, baby?

MADGE [*beseechingly*]:
I'm telling you, stay away. Now, please.

LARRY [*approaching MADGE*]:
And I'm askin' you a civil question. What the hell is goin' on?

MAX:
What's up, Larry?

LARRY:
She thinks I killed somebody—don't you, Madge?

MADGE:
Don't let him take me, Max.

LARRY [*grabbing her by the arm*]:
I mean she's had ideas before, doc, but not this kind. Come along, Madge. We're headin' home.

MADGE [*pulling away*]:
No!

LARRY:
No?

MAX:
Go easy on her, Larry.

LARRY:
Did she tell you that, doc—that I shot a guy named Charlie? She's been broadcastin' it up and down the whole goddamn street. I rubbed out a

212

guy named Charlie. Who's Charlie? I don't know no Charlie. Does she? Does anybody? Nobody tells me. I bring home a souvenir from some outta-hock store sale and right away I'm shooting up all the Charlies in town.

MADGE [*pulling further back as LARRY tightens his grip*]:
Max, please! Don't let him—

LARRY:
Did she tell you that, doc? I said, did she tell you that?

MAX;
Sure—sure, Larry. We don't know who Charlie is.

LARRY:
You see, baby, you're dreamin' again. Too much liquor, Madge. That's what it is. You should lay off the stuff.

MADGE:
Stay away from me, Larry. I'm warning you.

LARRY [*mockingly solicitous*]:
Madge.

MADGE:
I'm not going back, Larry, because I'm leaving.

LARRY [*forcing her off the bar stool towards the door*]:
You're leavin' alright. With me you're leavin'.

MADGE:
Stop him, Max! Stop him! He's got a gun.

MAX:
Naw, you're imaginin' things, Madge. He ain't got no gun.

MADGE:
You don't believe me? Wait for Bugs and Grace. They know who Charlie is.

LARRY:
We're waitin' for nobody.

MADGE [*pathetically*]:
Oh, yes—yes, I'm waiting for them.

MAX:
You better go, Madge. I don't want no trouble.

MADGE:
No, nobody wants no trouble. Then why do you lie?

MAX:
Lie?

MADGE:
All of you! You lie! You know who he is but you're all afraid of Larry.

LARRY [*forcing her closer to the exit*]:
Yeah, yeah, they all know. Come on, let's go, Madge.

MADGE:
But I'm not afraid—because I saw, I saw!

LARRY:
I said, get movin'.

214

MADGE:
He was shot—in the hollow of his chest. And he was shot again. And again. And again. Four times. And then everything went quiet. His heart, I could tell—it—it stopped beating. And I ran. A thousand miles I'm running—and no one can stop me—not even you, Larry. Now let me go!

LARRY [*shaking her violently*]:
Listen, Madge, there ain't no Charlie, can you understand? It's all in your head.

MADGE [*breaking loose, backing away towards the bar*]:
No, stop it! Killers, all of you! Killers! Killers!

LARRY [*advancing menacingly towards MADGE*]:
Crazy, that's what you are. Crazy!

MADGE [*she breaks the edge of the glass over the bar, spilling its contents*]:
Keep away. Keep away, Larry.

LARRY [*grabbing her left arm while trying to pry the glass loose with his free hand*]:
Drop it, or I'll twist you arm off.

[*MADGE manages to break free, aiming the broken edge of the glass at LARRY'S face, but inflicting only minor injury. An elevated train passes, causing a minor tremor.*]

MADGE:
He can't get me now, can he, Max?

LARRY:
You little whore.

215

[*Swinging violently, he knocks her to the floor, her head hitting the metal foot railing. Her purse falls beside her, spilling most of its contents.*]

MAX:
Christ, are you out of your head?

LARRY:
The damn fool, she cut me with the glass. You saw it.

MAX:
That ain't no reason.

[*QUEEN rushes over to MADGE, kneeling beside her.*]

QUEEN [*dabbing MADGE'S forehead with a handkerchief*]:
Madge—Madge, honey. [*To LARRY.*] See what you did, you clumsy—

MAX [*taking over*]:
Move away, Queen. Charlotte, get me a towel.

MADGE:
Get away, all of you!

[*The outburst is greeted with stunned silence. LARRY walks over and grabs her by the arm as CHARLOTTE returns with a towel.*]

LARRY:
Madge, you're comin' home.

MADGE:
Don't touch me!

MAX [*wiping blood from her forehead*]:
Leave her be, Larry. Can't you see she's bleeding.

[*Another silence broken by a chorus of gospel singers from across the street. MADGE reaches over and picks her comb up from the floor, then tries running it through her hair.*]

MADGE:
Where is the music coming from?

CHARLOTTE:
It's the tabernacle, honey. From across the street. There looking to save more souls.

MADGE [*running her fingers through her hair*]:
What happened to the nickelodeon?

CHARLOTTE:
It's still there. It's just not playing.

LARRY:
Okay, Madge, get up. We're goin' home.

MADGE:
It's too late now, Larry. I can't go home.

LARRY [*grabbing her by the arm*]:
We'll see about that.

MAX:
Take it easy, Larry. Can't you see, she's hurt.

LARRY [*lifting MADGE into his arms*]:
Everything's gonna be okay, baby. We'll get you to a doctor.

QUEEN:
I'm scared, Maxie. What does this mean?

MAX:
It doesn't mean anything. [*Heading for the street exit; to LARRY.*] Stay put, Larry. I'll get you a cab.

LARRY:
Everything was okay 'till she hit the street. I didn't tell her to come here. She came on her own. It's the street. It's the goddamn street.

MAX [*ironically*]:
You're right, Larry. It's the street. It's always the street. [*He whistles for a cab.*]

QUEEN [*offering MADGE her purse*]:
I'll tell Bugs and Grace that you were here. You want me to do that? I'll tell 'em you couldn't wait any longer—that you were going away.

MADGE:
They won't be angry?

QUEEN:
They'll understand, Madge.

MADGE:
What will be my reason?

QUEEN:
I'll tell 'em you were going away to see Charlie.

MADGE:
Charlie?

QUEEN:
That's a good enough reason. They'll understand.

MADGE:
Don't know any Charlie. Must be someone else you're thinking of.

MAX [*at the door*]:
Cabs out front, Larry.

[*LARRY exits with MADGE. MAX reenters to the sound of the cab pulling away. There is an uncanny stillness, broken only by the voices of the gospel choir that fade to background level and gradually out.*]

POP:
You know, there was a man once—came from Denver some years back. He used to like music. He couldn't play very well, but he liked it. And if I remember, he was all shot up, too. Used to come in once or twice a week just to see Madge. He was an odd duck, youngish sort. Could've been a lover, maybe even a son. Madge never talked about him much. Then one day, he disappeared—out of a clear blue sky, just disappeared, vanished. To where, nobody knows. [*A pause while he examines his glass.*] There's only one thing, though. [*Another pause as he pours the last of his beer into the glass.*] His name wasn't Charlie.

CHRIS:
What was his name, Pop?

POP:
I don't rightfully remember, but it was a good name.

[*He drinks up. MAX gets a broom and dustpan from back of the bar.*]

STREET VENDOR [*off*]:
Jesus saves. Jesus saves. Jesus saves.

219

MAX [*sweeping up the broken glass*]:
Queen, would you hand me the Racing Form.

QUEEN [*picking it up from the table*]:
Sure thing, Maxie.

STREET VENDOR [*standing in the doorway*]:
Jesus saves. Jesus saves.

MAX:
Some other time, pal.

STREET VENDOR [*he goes off*]:
Believe in Jesus for he is our savior…Jesus saves. Jesus saves. Jesus saves.

QUEEN:
Maxie, am I really the queen?

MAX:
You sure are.

QUEEN [*throws the Racing Form back on the table and sits*]:
Then get it yourself.

[*MAX picks up the Racing Form and returns to the bar.*]

POP:
Whaddaya say, Max? Am I good for another drink?

MAX:
Sure, Pop. Anyone with an educational background is good for another drink.

220

POP:
Make it three. I got a couple of friends with an educational background too.

CHRIS:
No thanks, Pop. We're leaving.

[*CHRIS and SKIP rise and head for the exit.*]

CHRIS [*to SKIP*]:
What's the matter, chum?

SKIP:
Nuthin', Chris.

CHRIS:
Then why so solemn?

SKIP:
I was thinkin' maybe the name ain't so bad. Maybe the street can get along with the name it's got.

[*They exit. POP slumps over, his head resting on the table, and passes out. His empty glass tips, rolls to the table's edge and falls to the floor. The nickelodeon returns as the scene dims to black.*]

www.ingramcontent.com/pod-product-compliance
Lightning Source LLC
Chambersburg PA
CBHW070104070426
42448CB00038B/1457